# FAT MAN

## ON THE

# LEFT

# FAT MAN

## ON THE

# LEFT

## Four Decades in the Underground

BY LIONEL ROLFE

*California* CLASSICS BOOKS

POST OFFICE BOX 29756, LOS ANGELES, CALIFORNIA 90029

❖

ISBN 1-879395-01-0

❖

Portions of this book have appeared in different form in the Los Angeles *Times*, the Los Angeles *Herald-Examiner*, the Los Angeles *Free Press*, the Los Angeles *Reader*, the Los Angeles *Daily News*, the *L.A. Weekly*, the San Francisco *Chronicle*, the San Francisco *Examiner*, the *B'nai Brith Messenger* and *Heritage*.

❖

Book and cover design by Deborah Lemattre.
Layout and production by Verna Flexon

*This book is for my mother, Yaltah Menuhin.*

# Acknowledgments

There were two main editors without whom this book would never have come together, although neither can be blamed for the final result. One of them, Woody Hoffman, is above. In this particular picture, he's the "Fat Man on the Left." Lionel Rolfe is on the right. Woody is an editor at City News Bureau in Chicago. John Ahouse, special collections librarian at USC's Doheny Library, is the other main editor. Nigey Lennon has also helped edit this manuscript, as have Nieson Himmel, Jeff Stalk and Mary Lou Aurelio. Phil Stern's photograph of the author ascending the steps to "heaven" in the old *Herald-Examiner* building adorns the cover. Paula Drucker and Karen Kaye were important friends during the coming together of this book. Much love to Bonnie Perkinson, who understands where this book is coming from. And without Israel and Imelda Baker, none of it would have been possible.

# Table of Contents

# Prologue

erhaps it is a conceit, but I feel uniquely qualified to write this book. I was born into a family whose story was one of the most archetypal of all California families. It was, I think, inevitable that I found myself headed down the road of California bohemianism. Whether I'm writing about terrible crimes or great scientific and literary movements, it comes too easily to me. There is something in my blood.

I'm as surprised as anyone at the stories that I come up with. More than once when I've started to look at all the things I've written about, I felt like a fraud. I'm just not that interesting a guy. I'm given to routine, and my internal weather usually revolves around nothing less mundane than paying the bills, sex, and my health. Yet the murderers and visionaries, the charlatans, warriors and peacemakers, the musicians and actors, the physicists and poets I've run across, their range is scary to contemplate. I don't necessarily think I've kept running across such people because I'm inherently fascinating; but my own story and narrative is odd and yet archetypal. There's magic at work, driving me ever along with the river's flow. I'm awestruck at whatever it is in my life that has worked out this way.

The first of the six books I've written was about the Menuhin clan. My uncle is Yehudi Menuhin, the violinist whose early career as a child prodigy was the 20th century equivalent of the Mozartian legend. Yehudi's two sisters, Hephzibah and my mother Yaltah, were child prodigy pianists as well. My mother gave her first concert with the San Francisco Symphony at the age of 10.

They emerged from the Jewish ghetto of San Francisco in the '20s. During the rest of the century they became a California archetype. Now Yehudi is Lord Menuhin, not just Sir Yehudi, and all his fond memories of what Mark Twain wrote about monarchy are now well hidden from view.

I've indeed grown up around legends.

This led me to other California icons. And ultimately to molding myself in the California bohemian tradition.

As a journalist, I have found myself strangely attracted to certain kinds of stories. It was out of my love for the great California bohemian writers like Mark Twain and Jack London that I wrote for the first underground newspaper in the '60s, the Los Angeles *Free Press*. Until I went to work for the *Freep* at the end of the '60s, my life had been as a wandering newspaperman through many of the byways and highways of the Golden State.

In the grand tradition of the wandering newspaperman, I had been fired from many a newspaper. Throughout the '60s I was blacklisted by the California Newspaper Association. I'd get a job, and then they'd find out that I had been a leftie in college. I got kicked off a number of jobs because they thought I was a communist.

Later I spent nearly a decade editing the *B'nai Brith Messenger*, the old Jewish newspaper in Los Angeles, which essentially ceased publication in 1996, when it was one year less than a century old.

I've worked for a newswire, covered lots of police beat, and written literary essays in the Sunday magazines of most of California's greatest newspapers. I won't say I've seen it all, because I know intellectually there's always more to see. But still I feel like I've seen a lot, and much of it is in this book.

I've made sense of my life during inspired moments that have occurred from time to time. These moments were intense and personal, and came about most often under a kind of shroud attached to a place, a circumstance or a room.

Running naked in the early morning fog of the golf park in Long Beach remains one of my strongest heavenly shrouds, a defining moment.

I stood alone in the forest. At least it looked like a forest at 5 in the morning. The meadows I saw beneath the enormous trees were only manicured grass. This was a particular place in Long Beach, a town south of Los Angeles. The golf course is still there, near Ximeno Avenue and Pacific Coast Highway. I delivered a newspaper route for the Long Beach *Press-Telegram* in the early mornings there, so sometimes on a foggy 5 a.m. morning I'd go to that golf course, with the great trees, take all my clothes off and run naked through the park. I don't think I was an exhibitionist, for I would have been quite embarrassed if I had run into anyone on these naked jaunts through the golf course meadow land with giant mysterious trees and the rolling fog.

There was a pastry shop, and when I went by it, trucks were pulling up to get the delicious sugary cherry turnovers they baked there. I always got one, because they were just baked and better than anything I had ever eaten before.

If my family conferred one central belief, it was that which was held most fervently by my uncle Yehudi: that white sugar is the enemy of modern civilization.

He may be right. But it's a poor substitute for Great Wisdom. I'll grant white sugar is bad for me, but it tastes so good. And pedaling my bicycle around Long Beach with 100 papers or so in the canvas bags over the rear wheels seven days a week, well, that was a lesson too.

In class struggle.

After a year, I was angry at the working conditions. I read Dickens; I knew that in many parts of the world young men my age were being forced to start working in mines for the rest of their lives. I knew that the faces of the Industrial Revolution are the faces that come of haunted, terrible grueling poverty and oppression. Mind you, even as a newspaper delivery boy, I knew that ultimately this would probably not become my plight. I was a son of the petit bourgeoisie.

I organized all the other paper boys. Then my boss, a large, red-faced Irishman with 12 kids, came to my dad and urged him to rein me in, saying that if I wasn't stopped, they were going to fire him. To sweeten the deal, the editor of the paper invited me to come downtown and have a tour of the newspaper plant—including the city room.

My dad the Judge understood class struggle; he had grown up in the Depression. But he told me I could no longer continue organizing the other paperboys. I think we got a raise of some sort. I got my tour of the building, and was very proud when a couple of my letters—I think they were praising Adlai Stevenson—-were published. It isn't that my dad was a reactionary. He pretty much remained a Roosevelt Democrat until his years of dotage when he became a kind of Reagan Democrat.

The experience injected ink into my veins then and there. The nicest thing I could say about the transition was that I had gone from organizing to educating.

That golf course was one of my first Inner Sanctums. But I had an earlier one. Like a man's first love, my first Inner Sanctum remains the prototype. When I was a kid, my parents used to put me on the Southern Pacific Daylight between Los Angeles in Southern California and Los Gatos in Northern California. Those trips back and forth between my parents and grandparents became very important to me. They were my first taste of freedom. Even today I occasionally ride the Amtrak Starlight, which is the same train as the old Southern Pacific Daylight, hoping to capture the memories of my first inner sanctum; those long, dark tunnels across the Cuesta Grade between San Luis Obispo and Paso Robles, the haunting dark green of spring's first moments of glory on the rolling hills just north of Watsonville. Racing alongside Highway 101, vestibule open and the wind blowing my hair, I was forced to squint my eyes until everything was a blur, hoping all the time that the conductor wouldn't show up and make me go back inside the coach.

When I got to my grandparents' house in Los Gatos, I went to sleep in the farthest bedroom from the main part of the house. It was a thick-walled, Spanish-style bedroom with windows that looked onto gigantic trees and the lawn on which I'd be playing by afternoon. In the morning, the lawn became shadowy and huge like a forest, particularly just before the sun came up. The steam engine of the San Jose-Santa Cruz train would come wailing and thundering across the nearby San Jose orchards, its revolving light searching the far corners of my bedroom. I could feel the steam hissing me back to sleep as the train sped on to its destination.

My grandparents' place was known as Rancho Yaltah and Yaltah is my mother's name. It was at Rancho Yaltah I found my first Inner Sanctum. It was my secret little room, there in the foothills of the Santa Cruz mountains. I read of things far away, and also listened to the birds and opened the window to the forest created by the trees on the front lawn. Again, perhaps the golf course was but a rekindling of this first memories at Rancho Yaltah, where I remember my thought processes beginning. There I first had childish thoughts of the sweep of evolution, past eras, the new ones that are coming, my family, who I was and who I was likely to become.

Now, of course, at the opposite end of my life I have traveled. Since my secret room at Rancho Yaltah, I have gone to Chicago, New York, London and Jerusalem. Like a first love, the secret little room, my Inner Sanctum, is now a more elusive place. Little of the innocence survives, and only the experience emerges.

Innocence is a state of grace. It is youth. It's the sweet mystery of life I used to contemplate as a kid when I lay in the bedroom of my grandparents' ranch home in Los Gatos and listened to the trains and thought about the world outside. When you're first discovering the world, it has few ambiguities. Everything is new and fresh and definite. Years later I lay on beds in dreary tenement housing that had to serve as my Inner Sanctum. I hardly noticed then that it was nowhere near as warm and friendly as the room in Los Gatos. My squalid abodes seemed glorious to me then, however, because I was caught in the prime of my adolescence. My parents had divorced, I was going to Los Angeles City College and working part-time as a library assistant, which meant I shelved books. I needed that money to live. I hadn't written much—just a novel when I was 16 that became the joke of the coffeehouse scene. It was called "The Red Blimp," and it had such memorable lines as "his balls hung huge and bigly." The first chapter was called "He for Whom the Sun Sat Down." I was reading a lot, a lot more then than I read now. I was reading Dostoyevsky and Romain Rolland, and writers like that.

I began fantasizing about my boss, older than I was but probably not by as much as it seemed then. She had long shapely, dark legs, and she was frequently on the other side of the bookcase shelf. She was a lightly-colored black, and that made her all the more mysterious and exciting. I couldn't tell if she was doing it purposely, but when she squatted down to put a book back in the shelf on the other side from me, I could see all the way up her legs.

After one such occasion, I walked into the back room, wondering if she knew that I was able to look up her legs. I thought maybe she would follow me into the employees' lounge.

No one immediately followed me. So I went into the bathroom, did my business, and when I emerged, there was a woman by the door. It wasn't my boss, however; it was a co-worker, a white girl from the South who had always seemed very quiet, very sedate—and I had not noticed, until then, how nicely built she was underneath her modest exterior.

I assumed a Southern Belle would never be attracted to me, or attractive. Her blouse looked mussed and open. For a shy, retiring kind of Southern Belle, she had a determined look in her eyes. She said nothing, but then she smiled, and again said nothing. When I reached for the door, mumbling something about having to go back to work, she placed herself in front of me.

She had the same last name as a famous U.S. Senator from the South, and she later told me she was a poor relation. That made the notion all the more exciting that I, a Jewish boy, was being invited to slip her bra and panties off. I knew I was giving the finger to the Klan, so to speak. Those were big days for the Civil Rights movement.

I went from the library and dark, dank coffee houses and such sordid pads of iniquity as the backrooms of libraries and bookstores directly to the newsrooms.

Over the years, I kept nearly everything I wrote in my various Inner Sanctums. I liked to be surrounded by the paper scraps, all that was left of my early newspapering experience. I began working on newspapers full-time when I was 19 years old. It didn't take too many years before the pile of newspapers was growing ever higher, ever rattier, never filed, and ultimately thrown away as garbage because they had become a fire hazard.

As I got older, there got to be too much paper to keep track of. Now if I need something, I have to get a copy of it from the file boxes of my writings kept in special collections at USC's Doheny Library.

But even if I can sometimes admit someone else has put a meaner pen to paper than I, one's own experiences are all one has. Memory goes very quickly, and putting it down in a newspaper is only a little better. Yesterday's newspaper rarely retains any of the excitement of the day it occurred. Paper yellows and gets old and crumbles. The most vivid events soon become grey yesterdays, that then continue to exist only out of the kindness of librarians who think it's worth preserving for a few years.

Also, I guess by the time you're getting on into your 50s, you don't have the right to be disillusioned about your family anymore. You shouldn't dwell on the subject all your life. But I can't help but have fond memories of those great enveloping shrouds of childhood from which my Inner Sanctum evolved. They felt real, more real than this City of Los Angeles I live in now. They're also old, and slipping away as I grow closer to death, but I think they'll last with me as long as I live. I know that how I saw the world as a youth was born of a lack of experience, but now that I have had some experience, I need to reach back and find out what those shining visions of youth were. Visions of Utopia on the hill began here; religious visions begun in Innocence, in an excess of Hopefulness.

By the time you've lived half a century, your view of the human condition becomes a little jaded. No one gets to live all the time among trees and parks. The urban jungle is always there, even if your roots were in some other place and time.

So my inner sanctums, my secret little rooms, wherever I have found them, could be nowhere else but California—they couldn't be in New York or Jerusalem. That's been true since I was a kid and the little room was at my grandparent's house at Rancho Yaltah.

The Inner Sanctum which I shared with my wife Nigey started failing as I grew older, but our six parrots kept this from being entirely so. Cleaning up after my birds is a pain, but they are worth it—for they stimulate my thought processes. They make me think of the sweep of evolution, of past eras, of new ones to come. In this little room I thought about a lot of things, and knew where I was and what I was.

The importance of this room where I sometimes lie and think, where I sometimes sleep and dream, and sometimes where my dreams are nightmares, has grown as Los Angeles has become an increasingly inhospitable place. From the windows of my room I saw the city afire during the great Los Angeles Riots of 1992. We saw the smoke from the stores on Vermont Avenue rising up into the sky. The television was blaring the news of the city caught in the grip of the riots, but by 2 a.m. we were too tired to stay awake. We had just gotten to sleep when reflections of flames began licking at our bedroom walls. At first I thought it was a dream, but it was persistent enough to force me to wake up. We both did, and then we saw a

house up the street suddenly burst into flames—and there were no fire-
men for such frivolities as a single housefire. Later we heard the fire had-
n't been set by roving gangs as at first we had imagined. Rather some old
drunk left a cigarette on fire, and burned himself and his house down, an
event presumably unrelated to the riots.

But watching that fire burning uncontrollably, we wondered if it
would just keep burning down the street right into the apartment we then
lived in. We already were trying to figure out how to put all the birds in
one car and get out of town. But get out of town where? And what streets
were there to the freeways that would be open? And who said the freeways
would be passable? Or gas stations open? Also, our car was old and not
entirely reliable.

Luckily the fire department did put out the blaze.

As I think of such scenes, I wonder why I stay in California. I have a
few friends, but my family is gone. I suppose it's that writers are part of a
priesthood, holding aloft the mirrors of truth, that keeps me where I am.

My Inner Sanctum, which is part my office, part my bedroom, part the
private space I reserve for myself somewhere in my brain, has survived
thus far, bloodied but unbowed. Through the vicissitudes, there do seem
to be constants. The two great California bohemian writers Samuel
Clemens and Jack London were among the writers who more than anyone
particularly made sense out of this world to me. I also read and loved
Henry Fielding, the great English episodic novelist, who preceded
Clemens by a century.

I have kept my Inner Sanctums from youth, when the world always
seemed an exciting world, full of promise and hope. Now the world seems
a bit more weary. But that is just part of the natural process of aging, I suspect. It's the same world no matter what end of my experience I'm looking
at it from.

My religion is the process of writing. Writing is my way of communing
with God, with Nature, whatever you want to call it. I am an atheist, so I
don't have to seek for the exact words as those who believe. For me, God,
Nature, these are at best literary metaphors for whatever framework makes
the most sense of things. I am in awe of the Universe. I worry about my
own species. I love a lot of the people and things around me, so I do not
want to lose the gift of life.

But I will one day, as will we all, and that's why I've written this book.

*The author, his mom, and his dad in uniform*

# Growing Up
# With Yehudi Menuhin,
# or How I Met Frank Zappa

he first time I lifted a bow to strings was in a junior high school class in West Los Angeles where I grew up. The teacher stopped me before the bow fell on the string and said to the five or six other youngsters there, "Look children. Lionel is the nephew of Yehudi Menuhin, who played the Beethoven Violin Concerto at Carnegie Hall when he was 10 years old."

I froze. Then I put the bow to string, and an awful screeching sound came out. That was the end of my career as a violinist. I ran from that class in complete and utter shame and never returned.

It was an inauspicious beginning to my musical career. My mother, a concert pianist, had tried to teach me herself. But she didn't have the patience, and I found myself suddenly unable to learn anything—even things I should have learned with no trouble.

So the decision was made to take me to other teachers. After the violin, I took up the classical guitar.

Three years later, I gave a little concert on the guitar. I played a piece by Sor. My right leg was like jello. I felt disembodied although the notes came out right. It's just that I couldn't have been making good music. After the polite applause, I decided then and there to give up music.

When I was about 16, I toyed with the idea of making films. I made an epic tied to the length of Smetana's "The Moldau," and it was all about the universe, the passage of time, and evolution. My biology teacher was so impressed with it, he had me show it before the entire student body in the school auditorium.

I realized that maybe Fellini and Eisenstein could make films that reflected their own intense vision, but that filmmaking was mostly the mechanics of bringing people together, organizing them and raising money. I decided to become a writer instead, because a writer never had to do much more than organize his own life and have a typewriter handy.

After my parents split up, I began hanging out in coffeehouses. It was the early '60s, and it was an exciting new world full of outlaw motorcycle types, newspapermen, communists, socialists, and social activists of all kinds.

***On the back of this picture, a doting grandparent had written,
"He plays the piano at 18 months."***

When I was 20, I went to work on a small town newspaper and for
most of the decade worked up and down the state as kind of a wandering
newspaperman—I thought I was doing so in the tradition of Mark Twain.

Thanks to the blacklisting efforts of the California Newspaper
Publishers Association, I was chased from one town to another. I had committed the terrible sin in my late teens of writing for the *People's World*, the
communist newspaper in California. By my 20s, I was not a member of
anything, although my politics remained on the left. I was just another soul
searching for the answer to who I really was.

That's how I came on my 29th birthday to be in London. It was
1971, and my mother Yaltah took me to the London premiere of a film
called "The Way of Light," which was about my uncle Yehudi and the
whole Menuhin family.

Yaltah made me wear a tuxedo, and we were chauffeured to the
theater in a Rolls Royce limousine.

We made our way into the inner sanctum of the theater, and as I
sat next to her there my mother was talking about me on the screen. She
was saying that she had not understood what a genius Yehudi was until she
had her first son. I froze, since she was obviously talking about me. And

*The author and his mother from an idyllic-looking scene on*
*West Los Angeles' Pelham Avenue in the '50s.*

suddenly all those frustrations about not being able to live up to her
expectations came back to me.

The next morning we had it out.

"You love your brother as if he were a god, the Messiah," I shout-
ed at her. Now I knew why I had spent so many years escaping the influence of my family.

My mother did not deny the charge, but added, "He is, after all,
a genius."

She showed me a book; on its cover was Schneur Zalman, an
impressive-looking gentleman who had been the Jewish equivalent of a
great guru. He was my direct ancestor, my mother told me, and the founder
of the Lubavitcher dynasty.

My first thought was, "Oh no, another Yehudi." The thought was
flip, but the moment was important.

As much as it hurt, I began clearing away the cobwebs of childhood ignorance to discover what exactly was the legend that so tormented and excited me.

When I returned to Los Angeles, I did not forget what had happened in London. A couple of years of intensive investigation followed during which I wrote a book. Yet the mystery remains. I never really found adequate answers. What is the source of great genius like that displayed in the Menuhin family line? What psychological factors foster an entire brood of genius children? Or is genius purely genetic, or prearranged by fate, or a miracle? There are no easy answers. I read everything I could find on prodigies in the psychological literature, which was surprisingly little.

It was also during this time I met Nigey, my future wife. She was cold, tired and hungry the first time we got together. She was 19 and I had just turned 30, and was living a relatively wild bachelor life in Hollywood. I had broken up with Dianna, my first wife and mother of my children, Heather and Haila. Nigey had no permanent place to live and was sleeping on a friend's couch. A short time before, she had been living in the basement of Frank Zappa's house on Woodrow Wilson Drive in Laurel Canyon where she had been a secret lover as well as a guest. But Nigey and Zappa also had an intense musical relationship. She watched the great musical cynic cry as he played her some Bartok, for example.

After a while, Frank's wife got upset. She knew he was not faithful to her, but she didn't appreciate it being thrown in her face. So Zappa prevailed on Ruth and Ian Underwood, musicians in his band, to put her up. Ruth was Nigey's closest friend at the time anyway. Nigey had also played guitar and sang in the band. So she was welcome to sleep on Ruth and Ian's couch. (Years later, when Ruth and Ian were splitting up, Ruth came and lived with us.)

One night she got in a fight with Ruth about something or other, and spent a couple of nights sleeping in her car. That's when I met her.

It happened that just before she came over to visit me I had read her cover story in the magazine where we both wrote. I fell in love with her writing. It was a biting, sarcastic and witty profile of a would-be rock star. So when we met in the editor's office the next day, and was introduced to her, I fell all over myself propositioning her, suggesting she come up to my place.

She did.

She was hungry. I opened a can of mushroom soup, which she devoured. I had some kind of meat leftovers in the refrigerator. After she was happily gorged, we went up to my bedroom—which was up a creaky flight of stairs to an attic bedroom in a woodsy house in Laurel Canyon. We lay down side by side, and with little discussion, made love. It seemed so simple and easy. It also felt something different than just passionate. It was incredibly comforting. I think for both of us. Ultimately, we became inseparable.

After we had lain there a while, the phone rang. It was a woman who regarded me as her boyfriend. I blurted out that I wasn't going to be seeing her anymore, that I had found somebody.

I hadn't even talked to Nigey about that. But she heard me on the phone—and she appreciated that.

I was ashamed of being so enchanted with a 19-year-old woman. But Nigey was different. She was so precocious, so bright, so interesting to talk with, so much fun, I easily forgot she was more than 10 years younger. I didn't feel that much difference between us at all. Mentally she seemed to be a wise old woman, and physically she was a young woman with great sexual appetites.

There was a rub, of course. She was still madly in love with Zappa, and would sometimes sneak away to see him.

Oddly enough, Zappa approved of Nigey and me and seemed to like me quite a bit. We argued about music. He was impressed by who my uncle was because Zappa wanted approval from the old European school—desperately, even if he constantly belittled the tradition.

I asked him what he would do with his electric instruments if the power went out. Turn on the generators, he smirked.

I was trying to make a point about the primacy of acoustic instruments, but it was ignored—by both Zappa and Nigey.

Sometimes Nigey's parroting of Zappa's musical views irritated me a lot. Perhaps my feeling was influenced by the thought that she still made love to him from time to time.

But I too had come from the wild '60s, full of Bohemian bacchanals and orgies. I liked the show of pulchritude that was around Zappa—so much the hallmark of Rock 'n Roll mythology.

When we got together, I'm sure that Nigey was also impressed with my being related to Yehudi Menuhin. In the '60s Yehudi made a series of records with sitarist Ravi Shankar called "East Meets West," and they were very popular. Nigey had studied with Shankar.

But she was also was hostile, since to her the Menuhins represented the old, the European. Classical music was that most unpardonable of things to her—snobby and unabashedly romantic.

Still, when I got a contract to write about my family, she accompanied me to London where we lived for nearly a year. She endured me not only listening to hundreds of my uncle's recordings as I prepared to write the family story, she also put up with my listening to Lubavitcher music endlessly. For an Irish-Greek girl, that probably was too much of a good thing.

The so-called Jewish music of the Lubavitch movement of Russian Jews had been invented by the founder of the father-to-son Rebbe dynasty in the 1700s. His name was Schneur Zalman, and his instrument was his voice. The Menuhins were Schneersohns and biologically I had as much right to be the Rebbe as the old guy who actually was.

Zappa's band came through London during the time we were there. Ruth called. We got tickets, went to the concert, and then got on the band bus. We got in a conversation with Jean Luc Ponty, the electronic violinist.

Nigey told him who my uncle was. He knew Yehudi's Bartok, which is indeed some of his best work. I asked him if I wasn't right to suspect that the electronics took away a lot of the essence of the instrument. Absolutely, he said. He conceded, frankly, that playing an electric violin reduced all the subtle nuances of the instrument to something kind of akin to a tinny, radio broadcast.

He said he gravitated to the electric violin just because of that. He said he knew he lacked something as a violinist, and the electric violin hid these shortcomings.

Nigey had a reputation as being a kind of wild woman. Once her father took me aside, and warned me that she wouldn't stay with me.

"She never stays with anyone. Gets bored too quickly. She'll move on," he said.

Several months later he again took me aside and admitted that I seemed to be the first man she was serious about. He said it sort of with a smirk that said he couldn't see what she saw in me.

Another person, a journalist, who knew her as part of the Zappa circle and knew the wild stories of Nigey at some of Zappa's after-concert orgies, offered her view of the apparent contradiction. At times Nigey had acted like the most wanton party girl, she said. But she also noted that Nigey was one of the most intelligent and talented women she had ever met, who could plunge into a deep conversation about philosophy at any moment. She also saw her perform on stage with Zappa at Carnegie Hall.

Yes, I knew of the discrepancies, and they made her seem wild and crazy and erotic beyond belief.

After the first trip to London, I had reason to become jealous of Zappa, because she would still see him. I was jealous of him, but I also genuinely could not see why people regarded him as a genius. Interesting and talented, perhaps. I thought Zappa's childhood friend Capt. Beefheart was more of an authentic genius.

One night shortly after we started living together, Nigey said she wanted to go and make dirty love to Capt. Beefheart.

Ever the '60s bohemian, I said sure.

I liked Beefheart. At that time, it didn't make me feel bad to think of her making love to him. People making love to others seemed the natural way to do things back in those still '60s-influenced days.

She came back that night and told me all about her session with Beefheart, and then we made wild love.

Later, after we were married, a little more decorum entered into these things. One night Beefheart called and asked her to drive out to meet him at the Denny's in Saugus. She asked if she could take me along, since we were now married. He grumblingly assented. All three of us stayed up eight hours until the sun rose the next morning and I think we got along well—just talking.

I felt as if I were living with a sex goddess, and what more, the sex goddess was in my corner. With her at my side—or so I felt—I slowly began to grasp the reality of Yehudi's incredible precocity on a yellow, smoggy day in Los Angeles. I was eating a hot dog in front of the UCLA research library, and I had just begun looking through some old news clippings of Yehudi's early life and exploits. I had been reading the perhaps overly zealous words of some of the awed reporters and critics who had greeted the boy violinist at the beginning of his career. Yes, there was something special about Yehudi. So special, in fact, that as I sat there eating that silly hot dog, tears came to my eyes. I tried to describe to Nigey what it was about the phenomenon that had so affected me. I now began to understand how seldom in history a child is born who can so move people that they abandon all pretense to anything but awe. Now I understood that while it might have seemed cruel, my mother was right to realize after having me that her brother had been a miracle. He was a miracle, or had been, and the shadow under which I had been raised was not just a shadow; it was something very real.

My eyes were full of tears of discovery, for I had also been learning much more about my ancestors, many of whom as children had been regarded as gurus and wise men. If they are my ancestors as much as they are Yehudi's, I thought, then some of their spirit must move in me. I was a product of a centuries-old tradition that had molded me without my knowing it.

I began a search of the psychology library and it soon became apparent to me that what science cannot easily quantify or prove it soon denies as a valid phenomenon.

One explanation offered up was that music is an area in which children can achieve exceptional success because music does not require experience in the way that writing and painting do.

But that is not true. When Yehudi was a 6-year-old boy, he played as if he had the wisdom of the centuries. People who heard him quickly realized this was not just superb technique, but someone who had an intellect and mind as profound as a sage.

I needed to begin my focused attack on the family history alone. Nigey would join me later in London.

I stopped at 790 Eastern Parkway in Brooklyn and met my "storefront rabbis" relatives whom my grandfather Moshe had always talked about. Once behind the first portal, I was submerged with feelings of deja-vu. Suddenly I understood where my grandfather's strange rhythm had come from. And now Hassidim emerged from the room where they had been chanting and davaning; they kissed the mezuzah on the door and went outside. I thought about how my grandfather had once been one of those worshipping, praying Jews; how I, too, in an earlier age, would have been one of them; how, even when one rebels, as had my grandfather, the effort is rarely completely convincing. No, I hadn't sprung from the air. I understood that now as I watched these Hassidim and remembered the childhood days I had spent with my grandfather.

When a thin, pale-looking Hassid had finished kissing the mezuzah, he looked straight at me, without giving me a sign of acknowledgment. He did not even ask me what I was doing there and left the building. Seconds later, another Hassid, with a more authoritative bearing, walked in the door and asked me what I wanted.

I heard my voice mumble something, and found I was being pointed at a door I assumed was an office. "Somebody should be there soon," a passing Hassid told me. Finally someone did come, an "American" rabbi. "Americans," as the Hassidim know them, are the younger generation who have stayed in the faith but were not born in Russia.

I began to explain my purpose to him, and he confirmed what I had been told by the Los Angeles Hassidic American rabbi, that Rabbi Israel Jacobson was the man I should talk to.

The "American" rabbi left, pointing to an extremely pale, delicate old man with a long, wispy flowing beard.

"No, no," said the yeshiva student who had suddenly appeared at my side. "That is the rabbi who deals only in questions of the Torah," he explained with unmistakable awe and reverence.

The "American" rabbi returned. He kept glancing up at me. Something was making him nervous. "Have you a yarmulke?" he asked. "Here," he said, handing me one.

I put it on. He looked relieved. "Yes, yes," he said quickly, and rummaged through a cabinet, coming up with a red yarmulke. I put it on, and the rabbi looked as if God Himself was smiling in His Heaven.

Now the Yeshiva student became very friendly. He wanted to talk. I asked him if he had ever heard of Yehudi Menuhin, the violinist.

"No," said the student. "Well," I said, suddenly feeling nervous, uncomfortable and out of place, "he's my uncle, and one of the world's most famous violinists. I'm surprised you haven't heard of him, for he is also a Schneersohn."

I talked for a while about the Menuhins and the Schneersohns, and about the book I was writing.

"I am related to the family, too," said the student proudly. I looked at him and saw that his broad, beaming countenance looked something like my own. I told him I had not been raised religiously; in truth, I hadn't even started to look into my family background until I had gone to London the first time. I hadn't know just how extraordinary and eccentric my family was. I had always known they were famous musicians, but not religious figures, too.

"I've been reading a lot about my ancestors," I said.

The student nodded.

We went down a narrow, winding stairway to a basement synagogue, a gigantic room filled with noise and hubbub. Everyone was chanting and talking; it was chaotic, and no one person seemed in charge. Even the student didn't quite know what to do with me. I spotted the "Torah Rabbi," and to my surprise, the student went up to where the rabbi was praying and interrupted him! The rabbi was surprised too, and angry. He glared at the student as if to say, "Deal with it as you will." So the yeshiva student returned to me and said I should put on tifillin, the Hebrew phylacteries. For the second time in my life, I did so. I repeated the Hebrew words without knowing what they meant.

That didn't seem to bother them.

Before I met Rabbi Jacobson, it had been suggested I live there in Brooklyn for a few weeks, just to get familiar with what I'd be writing about. I said it wouldn't be possible. On many levels that was most certainly the case.

The room where I met Jacobson was in a very unprepossessing, almost abandoned looking yeshiva building. I waited in a dingy room until he emerged from the inner sanctum.

At first he didn't understand my question, and my heart sank. Had I come all this way for nothing?

"Moshe Menuhin, my grandfather."

Jacobson still looked quizzical and I wrote the name down.

"Oh," he said. "Meshe. You're related to him? How are you related to him?"

"He is my grandfather."

"And what do you do?"

"I am a writer. I am writing a book. I am told we are related to the Schneersohns."

He nodded. "I have a letter," he said, "written to me from Russia many years ago about Meshe, the father of Yehudi Menuhin. Your grandfather is the direct descendant through a marriage with a daughter of the great tzaddik, Menachem-Mendel Schneersohn, the famed grandson of Schneur Zalman. And on his father's side he was the great-grandson of Levi-Yitzhak of Berditchev."

I knew who Levi-Yitzhak was. I remembered having read about the saintly but eccentric teacher, and saying to myself, "That man reminds me somehow of myself." Now I was learning that there might be a reason for this.

When I asked Jacobson to see the letter, he replied it was in Hebrew, and suddenly began to scowl—asking me questions like a prosecuting attorney. He wanted to know about my family, my upbringing and, of course, my Jewishness. When I said that my brother Robert was a physicist at Los Alamos, New Mexico, he asked "What's a physicist? Is that like a doctor?"

The more I described what a theoretical physicist does, the worse it got. I realized I would get nowhere talking about the relentless pursuit of the mechanics of matter, since Hassids are mystics who treasure all the mysteries as God's affair.

When I mentioned my daughter, he wanted to know if the mother was Jewish?

When I said she was not, he would not "besmirch the name of the

Schneersohns, one of the great of Jewish intellectual family names, by linking with that of the Menuhins. I will tell you no more."

I asked if he proposed I disown my own flesh and blood because their mother was a gentile?

Jacobson got softer and had an answer. That I stay in Brooklyn, living in the yeshiva. Or, he said, when I get to London I should look up Chabad, and stay away from the shiksas.

I knew I wasn't even going to begin to tell him about Nigey, my Irish-Greek shiksa goddess.

My next stop was Zurich, not London. In Zurich, I found my mother surrounded by friends who were deeply involved with the psychology of Carl Jung. The executor of the Jung estate was a very wealthy woman who supported the war in Vietnam. She was the main heir of Hoffman LaRoche, a large pharmaceutical house that also introduced LSD to the '60s with results that are well known. I sat on her couch and drank a lot of her very fine, I'm sure very expensive scotch and vodka, pissing her off and irritating my mother more. The drunker I got the more profane my language about Nixon became. The heiress was a big supporter of Nixon.

Still, I became drawn to the notion of a collective unconscious, of archetypes which Jung explains in part as a "certain psychic disposition shaped by the forces of heredity." Everybody I met in Zurich lived in houses built of stone in the 14th century, with only perhaps their wooden floors changed in all that time. Talk of archetypes made sense in such a surrounding.

My feelings about Jung were changed by my mother's new husband, Joel Ryce. He was in the process of becoming a Jungian analyst, and he showed me a book on archetypes, psychic symbols that have endured universally throughout man's history. In it, Jung talks of a natural and indispensable intermediate stages between unconscious and conscious cognition.

Jung seemed to be saying that it does not matter if myth is true or not—it just is. Myths tell us more about ourselves than does science or rationality, he says. Each of us has our own unique myth, yet we also have broad categories which he calls the child-myth. A child-myth is larger than any one child and yet it is the myth that molds all children.

Food for thought.

When I arrived in London, following my Zurich detour, my experiences in Brooklyn proved to be of great interest to Yehudi and Hephzibah. Yehudi said that "the tightness is the heart of their survival, the key to their survival. You must respect it."

Hephzibah grinned and said, "My God, they make Aba (the Hebrew word for "father," by which most of the Menuhins call Moshe) look like a tolerant man."

Yehudi told the story about the old Hassid listening to his grandson speak about the Red Sox and the White Sox. "Listen," the old man said. "Just answer me one thing. This Red Sox and this White Sox, is it good for the Jews?"

On another occasion Yehudi and I went walking through Highgate which was close to his house.

"Ten years ago," said Yehudi, "you didn't have all those ugly skyscrapers." We talked about squirrels, stopping to admire one scampering up a tree; and about the beauty of a particular, huge, almost purple tree. He spoke of the Hassidim. "It's a passion, a kind of lunacy. They are the kind of people who say, 'I'll be the best violinist in the world,' or 'The world has to be perfect,' even when it can never be. And they won't understand that it never can be, because between studying and praying they are not a part of the world. They are possessed."

As I said, I had been pondering Jung and his child myths. In a London library I came across the work of the French anthropologist Claude Levi-Strauss, and found in a passage about myth and music, the essence of which was that these are the two supreme mysteries science has not yet unraveled.

Levi-Strauss' words jumped out of the page at me, for suddenly I saw why I had found nothing satisfying about child prodigies, even though by now I had now searched for the answer in libraries halfway across the world.

Levi-Strauss suggested that the unraveling of the mystery behind music might be the key to a real scientific renaissance. Both music and myth, he said, operate in a continuum not limited by time. Both music and myth strike those chords in us which participate in that same inner awareness of timelessness.

Levi-Strauss sounded more mystical than scientific. The anthropologist said that his colleagues have been able to understand some of the mechanisms of myth as collective creations, but not those of music.

According to him, "we know nothing of the mental conditions in which musical creation takes place. We do not understand the difference between the very few minds that bring forth music and the vast numbers which do not, although nearly everyone is sensitive to music. The musical creator is comparable to the Gods."

I was just done finishing my research of Levi-Strauss when Nigey showed up. I had missed her sure, strong affectionate voice that so caressed my libido, my brain, my soul and my heart.

But Nigey was the opposite of all this religion stuff that had entered my studies. Suddenly I, an atheist, was writing about religious issues, which I usually saw as political issues.

A journalist friend suggested since I was related to the rebbes, why not set up shop, put me in a white robe with cabalistic symbols, and have done with it. He'd be in charge of the treasury and young women.

The man who founded the Schneersohn clan was, as I said, Schneur Zalman, who was the great *illuy*—prodigy—in religion and in song. Zalman's disciple was a man named Dov-Ber, and it was this Dov-Ber who was accused by some of having invented the Bal Shem.

And who, you ask, is the Bal Shem?

As my uncle was recording the Bach Brandenberg Concertos, I spent several hours in a room at the EMI studio with Princess Irene, formerly of the Greek monarchy, who had just come to live in London. She is related to British royalty, and spends considerable time with Yehudi and his wife Diana in London. At first I felt some resentment toward her because, unlike my uncle, I have no patience with the basic assumptions behind royalty. Yehudi really believes royalty adds something to a society. I think the whole concept a turnoff.

Yet I liked Princess Irene. When we talked, I quickly felt there was something very sad and discarded about her, that there wasn't an iota of bad intention in her, despite the fact that one couldn't say the same thing about her mother, the former Queen Fredericka, mother of the then recently deposed King Constantin, who also showed up to listen to Yehudi recording.

While Yehudi was out of the room, Irene asked me what my book was about and then told me she had learned of the Hassidic tradition, and she confirmed my thoughts when she said, "Yehudi's whole personality became clear to me and I understand who he was when I read Buber."

Irene also had been struck, as was I, by the uncanny similarity between the Hassidic wise men and the gurus of India. She told me when she discovered that Yehudi was descended from a generation of wise men, it was a revelation for her.

I went home and studied the album cover of East Meets West. As I studied the picture of Yehudi, looking like a wise man from another time, I thought I saw the Bal Shem flying across the mountain tops and sliding through the air on gusts of wind.

The Bal Shem was the great prophet of the Hassidic movement

that swept the Jewish communities in eastern Europe in the 18th and 19th centuries—the remains of which I had seen in Brooklyn.

The Bal Shem was born in 1700 and lost his parents while still very young. He was raised by the Jewish community in the tiny, obscure village of Okep. He lived at the heder, or school, but he rebelled against the heder and its musty rabbis and many arbitrary rules.

The Bal Shem's specialty was a state of mind; ecstasy or Hitlahavut. Schneur Zalman was committed to that, and so is Yehudi.

Through Hitlahavut the Messiah will be persuaded to come. Hitlahavut unites man with God in the wondrous state of concentration where even the most oft-repeated actions become fresh again.

The Bal Shem's mystics toured the Russian countryside, attacking abuses by the learned and teaching the common man that he could have religious power, much as Communist student revolutionaries would teach a couple of centuries later that workers could seize political power.

So who was the Bal Shem? No one knows. He left behind so many legends that all sense of proportion, of reality, has gone.

He is the figure at the bottom of the Lubavitcher dynasty legend, and hence also at the bottom of Yehudi's legend.

The Bal Shem was a gentle man. He and his wife lived in poverty at an inn in the Carpathian Mountains, but she was devoted to him. There in the mountains Hassidism was born. The Bal Shem spent many days alone in the wilderness, speaking the language of birds and trees.

A story is told that some bandits were waiting, ready to kill him as he walked precariously near a mountain cliff. He was so wrapped up in his thoughts that he was unaware of the chasm ahead. The bandits thought they would not have to do the evil deed after all; but then the mountains moved to bridge the chasm without the Bal Shem's even being aware of it.

After seven years in the mountains, the Bal Shem began to travel from village to village. He talked to the Messiah in heaven; when he traveled he traveled with the wind as his companion. He covered hundreds of miles through some other dimension than time and distance.

To hear him, they say, was to feel the magic of the sea and the stars, and to hear the soft stirrings of the air.

So what of all this is my Rosebud? What is genius? One doesn't have to be a genius to hear and understand music; but to make music, that is another thing. Still, maybe that genius is nothing more complicated than a state of mind. A state of mind cultivated by genes and religious impulse over the centuries.

I picked up my guitar and tried to play what I could still remember of the Sor etude. It wasn't much. It never had been much. And so I began crying.

When we returned, I finished my first book, *The Menuhins: A Family Odyssey*. It was good I did so, because it enabled me to move on past this Menuhin thing. The book was published in the late '70s.

When Zappa died in the early '90s, Nigey, who hadn't had any contact with him for most of that time, went into a deep funk.

Only once had we had contact with Zappa since the early '70s. We edited the old Jewish paper, the *B'nai B'rith Messenger*, then one of the city's pioneer papers. Zappa was having his war in the '80s with Tipper Gore, wife of the vice president, about her involvement with an anti-rock 'n roll group that thought the music was satanic.

The *Messenger* got involved because it turned out that the group Gore was involved with was also anti-Semetic.

I talked with Zappa a few times because on this story we were working with him.

He asked me if we both wanted to come up to his house for dinner, for old time sake.

For different reasons, we both said no.

When he died, though, I think Nigey rued that decision. His influence had stayed with her all those years, if not in body certainly in spirit.

I encouraged her to write a piece about him which ran in the London *Independent*. From that, she kept writing—day and night for several months—until she had finished her book, *Being Frank: My Time with Frank Zappa*.

Now she and Candy Zappa, Zappa's sister, are making a CD together.

And for me, the whole story of miraculous prodigies, and strange intense religious impulses that a family captured, seem no more. The miracles are no more. We end up in solitude, and then we die.

It is what is. Music elucidates it. Makes it concrete. Sees the beauty in it. That's why music makes things better, much more effectively, I think, than the holiest of the holies.

In the end, it's all just music.

*Author at 13 or so, already striking poses*

# Words Are Still Powerful

o do their work properly, words have to resonate with the milieu in which they were created. More than that, they have to communicate universally very much in the way that music does. I made a meager but soul-satisfying living for a couple of years waking up to days full of reading, thinking and writing about writers who lived in Los Angeles. This required location scouting as well as constant reclining in my Inner Sanctum, since it seemed to me that is how one learned about the writing that had been produced in a place. I wrote the book *In Search of Literary L.A.* out of the experience. Its chapters appeared first as pieces in the old and now-defunct *Herald-Examiner*, the Los Angeles *Times*, the Los Angeles *Reader*, and others.

As I worked on those articles and books, my life was truly centered in the Inner Sanctum. I rarely had to go to an office, except for a visit with an editor, or else to chase a check. L.A. was my word laboratory work. So please hear me out.

The reason why early dusk is so magical a time to visit literary Los Angeles is that it is a time of transition. Twilight is when the purple cloak of poetry dissolves the harshness of the everyday—a time when everything seems like ghosts flashing on the silver screen.

Time and place, you see, have been disappearing characteristics in the modern fiction coming out of New York for decades. But in Los Angeles time and place are still the stars of our dramas. Maybe time and place are but ephemeral phenomena, in life and to a lesser degree in literature—maybe both are but a writer's conceits, constructs, facile artifices. But the fact is that Los Angeles has put its garish mark on world literature with them. Desert sun and hillside brushfires have given this place its own luminescence. The fires of Los Angeles are primeval, from the very bowels of the earth.

Try to spend most of the early dusks near a literary L.A. landmark. Then you will see that this is a harsh but beautiful place, over which a thin veneer of civilization has been laid, but that is what gives L.A. writing its robustness.

Go first across the pass through the Los Angeles basin where the Santa Susanas and the San Gabriels intersect, where the freeway interchange of the 5 and the 14 has collapsed not once but twice in earthquakes over the last two decades. If you spent any time on the other side of the basin, you could have watched the great red fires sweep out of the hilly canyons every summer, and contemplate the ravens and other great birds who circled the nearly lunar desert landscape where you expect dinosaurs to be roaming and pterodactyls to be roaring and wobbling through the air.

Here, just the other side of the Los Angeles metropolitan sprawl, you get to feel the rhythm of the fires in summer and the torrential rains, floods and occasional snows in winter, and dread the inevitable punctuating earthquake. The Mojave Desert starts just the other side of the basin, and with sufficient exploring you'll see where giant rock structures have dramatically uplifted the earth's violent geology. It is tentative, primitive land in either direction—and it's the same land really that you find inside the basin, only there it has been covered over with the appurtenances of the city.

As dusk sets in, plan your return through the basin wall from old downtown Newhall. Just before you get to the freeway entrance to Highway 14, turn right on the old road instead and on your right you will see Eternal Valley Cemetery. It was right on this spot where the old Butterfield stagecoach inn, called Lyons Station, stood until it burned in the early '20s. Samuel Clemens came as close to L.A. as he ever got in the early 1860s here, and supposedly signed the Lyons Station register. Twain might have spent but an hour or a night here in the 1860s, not far from the future great city of Los Angeles; but the city would not remain untouched by the the first pristine California bohemianism he represented.

California bohemianism had a hard time competing with the terrible apocalyptical mood and writings in Los Angeles of Aldous Huxley, Malcolm Lowry, Nathanel West, Thomas Mann, and others who came with the cataclysm in Europe that culminated in the Holocaust. Charles Lummis institutionalized California bohemianism in Los Angeles when he erected El Alisal, the stone house he started working on before the turn of the century along the arroyo, now off Avenue 43 off the Pasadena Freeway. But you can get an even better feel for it in Hollywood by visiting the house at 5152 La Vista Court, an obscure alley off Van Ness in the first block south of Melrose Avenue. The rickety three-story building used to have a blue enameled inscription, "Jack London Slept Here" beneath a bas relief of Jack London. The bas relief is still there, but the plaque was taken down by its owner Bob Gary. Most of the structure was built in the early '20s by sculptor Finn Frolich. Frolich was a close friend of London's, and designed and sculpted the busts of Jack London that still decorate London's Valley of the Moon Ranch, now a state park, just north of San Francisco, and the entrance to Jack London Square in Oakland. Frolich built his house around an earlier structure, that now forms the rear of the building, where London may have stayed near the turn of the century when he came south to Los Angeles, usually to buy cattle for his Valley of the Moon Ranch—supposedly, as we already mentioned, on the cattle lot where the Silver Lake Reservoir was later built. What is known for sure is that George Sterling, another of London's friends, known as the patron saint of the California bohemian movement and the prototype for a major character in London's *Martin Eden*, spent time here. The place was a veritable Southland hangout for some of the most famous of California bohemians—and if Gary, who also is a bohemian soul, is around and sociable, you might get a fascinating tour.

Perhaps the greatest single moment of bohemian influence in Los Angeles was through Robinson Jeffers. We took a hike to the ghostily remains of White City, which is up near Mt. Lowe. You have to walk because even the track of the train that used to run up the hill back of Altadena is gone now. Still the roadbed is there. It was at the top of Mt. Lowe at the turn of the century where the poet Robinson Jeffers first proposed marriage to Una Kuster during a romantic interlude, replete with a detective the lady's unfortunate husband had hired. Jeffers later became the legendary poet who wrote his great epic narrative poems from Big Sur, where he worked in a stone tower on the seaside that he built himself by hand. But at the point he met his future wife, he had backpacked all over the San Gabriel mountains while a student at Occidental College. When he wearied of the mountains or of the urban blight he felt existed even then (he lived at 1623 Shatto Place), he lived for a while in Hermosa Beach where he would get drunk with the sailors from the schooners that still docked there, took long solitary walks on the beach and cultivated his passion for birds, wind, and Mrs. Kuster, who eventually became his wife.

Like the powerful socialist movements that had built up before the First War, California bohemianism was done in by the war, then the Great Depression and finally World War II. The noonday sun and even its concomitant dusk took on a harsher reality in the apocalyptical writings this place produced. At once frightening and compelling, the unstinting heat and the fires were the inspiration for Nathanael West's *Day of the Locust*. He wrote the book during a summer he spent unwell and financially pressed in a Hollywood boarding house at the height of the

35

Depression. If you walk up the steep incline on Ivar Street just north of Yucca, you'll find the Parva-Sed Apta apartment hotel, the block's oldest structure, a cross between Tudor and Black Forest cottage style. The heat of the summer sun and the deadly red from the brushfires in the nearby Hollywood Hills, colored West's perceptions of L.A. forever. Throughout *Day of the Locust*, his protagonist, a movie-studio artist, is working at home on his masterpiece, "The Burning of Los Angeles." As West explained, "He was going to show the city burning at high noon, so that the flames would have to compete with the desert sun. ...He wanted the city to have quite a gala air as it burned." At dusk, the shabbiness of this part of Hollywood will look a little less extreme—it doesn't have to look that much less extreme, because even in the '30s when West lived at the Parva Sed Apta, writing *Day of the Locust*, there was still plenty of urban blight around.

The most apocalyptic of all writers surely was Malcolm Lowry, who wrote *Under the Volcano*, a cabalistic descent into the underworld on the fiery verge of World War II, in a room at the Hotel Normandie that's now a retirement home at Normandie and Sixth. The protagonist, the Consul, ultimately disappears into the molten heart of Popocatepetl in Mexico. Lowry met and married Margerie Bonner, who became his lifelong companion and unnamed co-author, at the street car stop in at the corner of Hollywood and Western boulevards in 1938. Early dusk may  not be such a bad time to contemplate this piece of literary history, but the nature of the neighborhood is such that you might not want to hang around in literary reverie there once dusk turns into night.

Thomas Mann wrote his great satire of early 20th century composer Arnold Schoenberg, whose son Ronald is a municipal judge, the same municipal judge who let O.J. Simpson off with a relatively light sentence on a wife-beating charge. Schoenberg (the elder) was a problematical musical presence in Los Angeles in the '50s, nonetheless he ended up getting honored with buildings and institutions at UCLA and USC.

The sun, light, and fire of L.A. heavily influenced European literature in the case of Thomas Mann's *Doctor Faustus*. Regarded as maybe the greatest European novel of the 20th century, it never mentions L.A., but still it was conceived and written here while Mann was living at 1550 San Remo Drive in the Pacific Palisades, not far from Schoenberg's Brentwood residence at 116 N. Rockingham Ave. The novel concerns the decline of Germany into barbarism during World War II; its protagonist Leverkuhn—the Schoenberg figure—was a metaphor for Germany's sickness. Mann was inspired to write as the result of a childhood vacation he took in Palestrina, Italy. He disliked the palm trees and blue skies of Palestrina for being so un-German, and years later, forced into exile on the Pacific coast, the bright sun of California and its infernal palm trees threw into relief new dark thoughts about his homeland.

Perhaps the most telling of all dusk literary trips is to go out Highway 14 to Pearblossom Highway, also known as State Highway 138, to Llano, five miles east of Pearblossom. The North-South main drag of Llano is 175th Street, and after the pavement ends and the gravel begins you'll see, to your right, behind a fence, the old ranch house where Aldous Huxley lived when he left Hollywood in 1942 and moved to the Mojave desert. The house was on the eastern boundary of the old utopian Llano colony. Huxley began writing *Ape and Essence*, about the aftermath in L.A. of a nuclear holocaust that was preceded by "three bright summer days"—his characterization of the great flashes of light from the nuclear bombs. Hiroshima and Nagasaki were on his mind as he wrote this book, and he was nearly blind at the time. Light had become his obsession. He believed that the desert light enabled him to see more, and he even drove his car across the desert floor, convinced he could see more clearly because of the direct desert light and distinct shadows that came with dusk.

The two major hot spots of literary bohemia in Los Angeles were in Echo Park as far back as the '20s and Venice in the '50s. I remember the late Jake Zeitlin, L.A.'s most famous bookseller, describing that scene. He explained why bohemianism flourished in Echo Park: "The rents were low, the shacks on the tree-filled hills afforded more privacy than flatland apartments did, and people could conduct their individual lives in peace. Bohemianism thrives on adversity. You have to have a concentration of people practicing their arts, people with superior endowments who don't necessarily fit into society, and who are, in fact, often engaged in rebellions against convention, creating a symbiotic society where not only can they go and eat at each other's houses when they're hungry, but where they can also spark each other and be each other's critical audiences. To such people, money is not the main motivation; they may like spaghetti and wine and conversation and not getting up in the morning to go to a job, but all believe in practicing something that is their justification for being, whether it be dancing, writing, sculpturing or music."

And what a group of people Zeitlin belonged to in Echo Park— his everyday friends included people like poets and writers Carl Sandburg, Carey McWilliams, and Louis Adamic, photographer Edward Weston, composer John Cage, filmmaker John Huston; and Sadakichi

Hartmann, the half-German Japanese who had been the very archetype of bohemianism in the early days of Greenwich Village and had introduced Japanese printmaking to the United States.

South of Sunset Boulevard and Echo Park Avenue, at the north end of Echo Park Lake, there's a great exotic lotus plant collection. It was put there by Aimee Semple McPherson, close to Angelus Temple which she meant to be the mother church to the 4,000 churches of the international Foursquare Gospel movement in 1923. The charismatic McPherson led the great religious movement until she faked her own disappearance to hide the fact she was having an affair with a young man. McPherson was widely known in the Echo Park bohemian circle of the '20s, because she was a woman of voracious sexual appetites. Hanging out amongst the Bohemians enabled her to have these satisfied without disillusioning the good plain folks who made up her congregation.

If you drive north up Echo Park Avenue until the street narrows at the top of the hill, and winds in and around the top of the hill over-looking the train yards, you'll be in the area where a lot of the action was—in the '20s and in the '60s. Almost all the houses at the top of Echo Park Avenue still fit Zeitlin's description of Echo Park in its bohemian heyday in the '20s. At dusk, among the ghostly trees and the wooden hill-side bungalows, it's easy to imagine life on the hilltop. In what was one of his sweetest memories from long ago, Zeitlin described how "Someone had tied a long rope with a tire to one of the trees at the end of Echo Park Avenue, so you could stand on one side of the little canyon there, grab hold, and swing out over it, describing a sort of semicircle. If you were lucky you'd land back on the hill. One night when Carl Sandburg came visiting, and the moon was bright, and we had imbibed a considerable amount of good wine, we went walking up toward the trees. I reached out and grabbed hold of the tire and swung out. I had no idea he was going to do the same thing—as soon as I got back, Sandburg gave a Viking war whoop, grabbed the tire, swung out over the canyon, and managed to get back to the other side without falling off." On another drunk, full-mooned night at the top of Echo Park Avenue, Zeitlin remembered walking along a ridge and seeing a naked woman coming toward him. He called out to her, but she dove off the side of the road into the bushes. He called her again, but she had disappeared. He continued walking toward the house from which the sounds of a party were emanating, and from which the naked woman apparently had come.

If you take a stroll along the Venice boardwalk at dusk, you can almost be transported back to the '50s when this was the headquarters of the great beatnik scene popularized by Larry Lipton in his best-selling book *The Holy Barbarians*. The condos, the yuppies, and the circus-like atmosphere that have made the boardwalk an internationally famous promenade in the last couple of decades are not so visible on the boardwalk at dusk. The weekend visitors and television cameras are gone—all that is left behind are the residents and drunks—more the way it was in the '50s. A lot of the original buildings of the '50s scene are still extant. One of the most famous coffee houses was The Gas House, on the southeast corner of Market Street and Ocean Front Walk. The building, an old bingo parlor, has been torn down, but one pillar still stands. Another popular spot was the Venice West, at #7 Dudley Ave. The beatniks traveled back and forth between Venice and San Francisco, but the Venice scene did produce poets Stu Perkoff, who was the original proprietor of the Venice West, and John Thomas, who still writes poetry and lives in Venice near the boardwalk with his wife Philomene Long, a writer who variously describes herself as "the beatnik nun" or the "retired queen of bohemia"—"retired" because she has a regular job these days.

While Venice in the '50s got all the attention, Echo Park and Silver Lake actually had more "beat" residents. An active coffeehouse scene was extant in the vicinity of Los Angeles City College by the late '50s, with such hangouts as the Viteloni, Xanadu and Pogo's Swamp attracting frequent visitors such as Dorothy Parker of Alguonquin Round Table fame, Christopher Isherwood and Mort Sahl. Eric Nord, the San Francisco poet who operated the Venice West, was one of those living in Silver Lake in those days of beatnik glory, as did Gregory Corso, Phillip Whalen and Michael McClure.

The Xanadu, just next door to the Lithuanian Cultural Center on Melrose Avenue, around the corner from Los Angeles City College, closed in 1963, and many of the old crowd went to the Fifth Estate at 8226 W. Sunset Boulevard in whose basement Art Kunkin began the Los Angeles *Free Press*, the "underground" paper that was the granddaddy of such "alternative" papers as the L.A. *Weekly*. If you walk a block or two east on Sunset Blvd. where there's now a McDonald's near Crescent Heights, that's where the old Garden of Allah hotel was. Dorothy Parker, Robert Benchley and F. Scott Fitzgerald, among others, held forth here in the '30s and '40s.

I spent a night drinking in Hollywood bars with Charles Bukowski, who was perhaps the greatest of specifically L.A. writers. The best of those bars are gone now, as well as many of the fleabags in Hollywood and certainly on old Bunker Hill where Bukowski lived. But if

you just look to your right, look to your left, you see the winos, the home-
less, the crazies, the just plain down and outers on the streets anywhere in
L.A. these days, on almost any of these corners Bukowski probably stood,
inhaling the perfume of urban decay at dusk.

# Politics of Innocence

lease understand me, it isn't that all virtue resides on the Left. I've met some really awful people who claimed to be Leftists, and some wonderful people who were, if not reactionary, privileged and conservative. Moreover, they were far more honest human beings than the Leftists I knew with whom I shared my politics. When they said they'd do something, their word was good. If they said something wasn't true, especially if they knew it from their experience and not their ideology, it probably wasn't true.

Nonetheless, I still adhere to a vision of things that includes the premise of human progress. Looking at things as scientifically as we can, and conducting our public affairs in the most democratic of terms, are basics of any progressive outlook. We have the ability to ennoble ourselves, as well as to grovel with the most debased of our instincts. The Free Market debases the best in our culture, and at its worse will lead to the horrors of fascism.

But there was also the Gulag.

It was socialism's misfortune to have had its first trial run in the Czar's Russia. Had socialism evolved in Germany—where it almost triumphed over capitalism, but instead failed, opening the way for fascism— history would have been quite different. Thousands of socialists were elected to office, including the mayorships and councilmanic posts of some good-sized American cities, in 1912. I have written the story of how socialism and organized labor were then defeated by General Harrison Gray Otis and his Los Angeles *Times* in *Bread & Hyacinths: The Rise and Fall of Utopian Los Angeles.* I believe that the combination of socialism and democracy, based on a rationalist, scientific base, would have turned the United States into a paradise.

But I promise no cheap philosphy here. A big part of me would like to do what Rush Limbaugh does, and proclaim my views to the millions. But even if I were as articulate and slick as he is, which I'm not, it would never happen. The left has been barred from national dialogue in this country for now. Still, I'll give Rush Limbaugh some ammunition with which to attack me. I'll tell you about my times in the Communist Party.

In the '50s and '60s I grew up as the essential West Los Angeles kid, but I was always fascinated by small-town America because that was where the soul of the country is. The Los Angeles where I grew up in the '50s was a smaller place than it is today, not in land mass but in population. Besides, as a young man, I spent most of my summers and winter vacations at my grandparents' house in Los Gatos. Los Gatos was a small northern California town near San Jose, and in my childhood it was characterized by orange orchards, not Silicon Valley industries. There was an old fashioned Greyhound bus depot, thriving because the train from San Jose to Santa Cruz with a stopover in Los Gatos had ceased running not too long before. There was a bakery, a fruit and vegetable stand, and a butcher, and the proprietors knew their customers by name.

In the same way West Los Angeles has metamorphosed from modest suburbs to megabuck enclave, Los Gatos is a very upscale place today. Then it was just a small town like a lot of other small American towns. The suburbs springing up out of the orange orchards were peopled by blue-collar Americans; you might remember Kerouac writing about Los Gatos after visiting Neal Cassady there, who had worked on the Southern Pacific Railroad. Cassady was no longer working on the railroad by the time Kerouac visited him in Los Gatos. He was working in a body and fender shop.

Los Gatos was just over the Coast Range from Carmel and Big Sur. I also spent time in Carmel and Big Sur during the '50s, although I was definitely too young to be hanging out with beatniks. My mom, however, was a kind of '20s bohemian at heart, which helped me pick up on the beat Zeitgeist. Carmel was essentially settled by turn-of-the-century bohemians right after the 1906 earthquake.

Despite spending time in Northern California bohemian and beatnik haunts, however, I remained essentially a Westside Los Angeles kid. Most of what I really knew of small American towns I learned reading Sinclair Lewis, and then Willa Cather, who, because of my mother's friendship with her, was my godmother. My mom never had any money to give me, but she did give me the letters Willa Cather had written to her—letters which academics had been pestering her for. The letters are now at the Cowboy Museum in Oklahoma. I didn't get rich from the sale, but I had enough to live for two or three months.

In Los Gatos as a young man, my grandfather Moshe introduced me to the written word. His were much more political than literary or philosophical concerns, and I'm sure he would not have been at home with beatniks. But his influence on me was great. Moshe faithfully read two publications all his life, whatever part of the world he found himself in. He had the daily and Sunday *New York Times* flown in—he was proud of the fact that the *New York Times* itself had commended him on being one of their most loyal customers—and he never missed an issue of The *Nation*. He explained to me that The *Nation* had begun as an abolitionist journal, which of course piqued my interest because there were increasing signs in the '50s of the great civil rights struggles that came to a head in the '60s. When Moshe first came to the United States from Palestine in 1916, he fell in with the Industrial Workers of the World, the Wobblies, whom he revered with almost the same passion he revered the American flag, which he did with an immigrant's uncritical gratefulness. But even "good" Americans knew about Upton Sinclair and Jack London—these were the two writers who radicalized whole generations of Americans and millions more around the globe.

I definitely was one of those who came to the Left as a result of reading. And I still believe in the primacy of the written word; most everything of value I ever learned was in printed form. The writers I was attracted to, beginning with Mark Twain and Jack London, and continuing on through Sinclair Lewis and Upton Sinclair, John Steinbeck and Carey McWilliams, and with diversions abroad to folks like Sean O'Casey and Romain Rolland, were all men of the Left. You couldn't be worth your salt as a writer unless you were a critic of the establishment. That seems to be the nature of the beast, with the one great exception of poet Robinson Jeffers, but I have written of them elsewhere so I will not dwell on that matter here.

I suppose it is a testimony to Moshe's influence that so much of the reading that attracted me was about injustice. Like every good schoolboy of an earlier generation, I read Charles Dickens and Mark Twain, and later Alan Paton's *Cry The Beloved Country* and Upton Sinclair's *The Jungle*, Jack London's *Martin Eden* and *The Iron Heel*, and Sinclair Lewis's *It Can't Happen Here*. I also read George Orwell and Aldous Huxley. The war against fascism was still only a few years past when I was a young boy, and Nazism is injustice by definition. I'm afraid the fact that the staunchest fighters of fascism were those who called themselves communists counted for a lot.

Definitely an important consideration in my commitment to the political Left was learning about anti-Semitism. One day (I don't remember why), my mother picked me up from school and we flew up north to visit her family, but stayed this time not at her parents' but at Alma, her brother's estate in the Santa Cruz mountains. While there I read a book published by the United Nations, under the sponsorship of two famous Jews, Albert Einstein, and uncle Yehudi. I discovered the Holocaust book on the shelf at the Baller Cottage at Alma. It was there I learned the details of the Holocaust, the dreadful creation of the graveyard that fascism had made for millions of Europeans, Jews and non-Jews alike, but mainly Jews. Baller Cottage was named after Yehudi's musical associate, pianist Adolph Baller. When Baller was in a concentration camp, the Nazis asked him what he did for a living. He said he was a pianist. So the Nazis took out their hammers and broke all his fingers. Baller always stayed in this cottage when he came to Alma, so that, obviously, must be added to the picture.

For professional reasons, my father had to move to the port town of Long Beach to take an appointment as a workers compensation appeals court judge there. In those days, Long Beach still betrayed its Midwestern roots, with its Iowa picnics, and the concomitant fact—to my mind at least—that there were still many followers of Gerald L. K. Smith around who blamed everything on the Jewish conspiracy. Since I was Jewish, I wondered why I hadn't known about this conspiracy.

Along the way I had discovered a book that I read and then reread a number of times because it seemed to explain what was puzzling and appalling to me in Long Beach. The book was Sinclair Lewis's *It Can't Happen Here*, the tale of a Hitler-like American named Buzz Windrip and his "Corpo" followers who stage a fascist takeover in this country during the Depression. The book was written during the rise of Mussolini and Hitler in Europe. Things happened to me in high school that focused the question. A Christian minister's son and his gang of thugs used to chase me home, south to Belmont Heights through the back alleys from Woodrow Wilson High School, howling the epithet "Christ Killer" and *Kike* and such other terms of endearment. My two best friends had last names like Garrison and Austin; one's father was a commercial fisherman, the other a career naval officer. Mr. Austin, my friend's father, had two mentors in life—Gerald L.K. Smith and Henry Ford. He would sit and tell me about the Jewish conspiracy for hours, and I listened because I assumed this was the way all gentiles thought. He also hated the "Japs," because even in those days it was becoming difficult for American tuna fishermen, who were usually—like Austin—independent entrepreneurs competing with the floating tuna factories that the Japanese used. I started becoming militant about my Jewishness. I decided it was not something I was ashamed of, quite the contrary. I was also a budding atheist as well, and forced attendance at the Christian assembly, with its story of Jesus the Messiah, was insulting to Jews—after all, it was in his name that anti-Semitism was invented by the Romans. I explained my opinion to the boys' vice principal at Woodrow Wilson High School. The principal ordered me to attend the Jesus assembly, because "this is a Christian country," and I had best accept that and shut up with this Jewish stuff.

My parents separated and my father and I moved back to Los Angeles when I was 16. I no longer lived in West Los Angeles, however. We moved to Hollywood, which was an exciting place in the '50s and early '60s. The changes coming in American society were palpable. The famed San Francisco street poet and self-proclaimed "Albanian Communist" Jack Hirschman was still then only an English literature instructor at UCLA, who gave great seminars on James Joyce that drew standing-room-only crowds. The coffeehouse scene in which I came of age had moved from Venice to Hollywood, Echo Park and Silver Lake. The coffeehouses often served as a staging area for whites and blacks going south to engage in civil disobedience.

In the early '60s, I became a member of the Communist Party in Southern California. While trying to integrate a housing tract in Torrance, I went to jail with Jerry Farber, who wrote *Student as Nigger*. Not that Farber, quite a well-known figure at the time, was a communist; I don't think he was. But he summed up a lot of what was motivating me politically. There was something peculiarly exciting about being in a jail cell with Jerry Farber and I don't remember what we talked about it, but I'm sure it was the stuff of those heady '60s years.

During the '30s, there was hardly a writer of any substance who did not grapple with the party's existence and meaning.

By the time I joined the party, it had been decimated by McCarthyism. Still, I found in it a link to the vitality of the past that I had already discovered in books. The party still published the *People's World* in San Francisco, which was like its sister paper *The Worker* in New York. Or it was supposed to be like the *Worker*. As it happened, the *People's World* always had a more independent line than the *Worker*, and was also a much better written paper with a surprising large readership and influence. There was no underground or alternative press then.

I didn't stay in the party long, but to say it didn't affect me would be wrong. The American Communist Party was a very real part of California and American history, whatever the present state of its existence. I was one of a great many radicals of the '60s who were deeply affected by Dorothy Healey, the chair of the Southern California district, which after New York was the biggest center of Communist Party activity in the country. Ultimately, Dorothy left the party, and is now spending the last decades of her life in the company of social democrats rather than communists. Her memoirs were published by Oxford University Press, because her history has been the history of California as well, especially her years during the *Grapes of Wrath* era in the Central Valley.

I was only 16 when I began trekking down to 84th Street in the heart of the black ghetto to visit Dorothy and talk politics. She was always was ready to answer my most difficult questions with interesting, thought-provoking answers, and ideas and information that seemed genuine and significant.

Through Dorothy I also met people like her former husband, Slim Connelly, who had been the West Coast president of the Newspaper Guild when Heywood Broun was president in New York. I got to know Al Richmond, editor of the *People's World*, who had been responsible for hiring Woody Guthrie as a columnist. I used to be at Dorothy's when Richmond would show up, sit down, and start drinking. He was a hard-drinking man, and also a hard-writing man. He did both well.

Ultimately Richmond wrote *A Long View From The Left: Memoirs of an American Revolutionary*, a most important book. Through the *People's World*, I also got to know Alvah Bessie, one of the Hollywood Ten, who encouraged me in my writing more than anyone had to that point. I also loved some of the reporters on the *People's World*. Steve Murdock made beer in the hallway of his Berkeley home, where I sometimes stayed, and wrote about sports for a sports magazine that appreciated him enough not to care that he was writing about California politics for the *People's World*.

I liked the *People's World* so much that I used to go around California with other comrades selling it. I remember in particular one time selling the *People's World* in front of the California Democratic Council convention in Fresno. The CDC was a grassroots Democratic Party organization that had a certain radical tone given to it by the fact that so many of Upton Sinclair's End Poverty in California cadre from the '30s had migrated there. The CDC was mostly Roosevelt Democrats, a lot more conservative than the socialists and communists. But in Fresno, I found out that all factions read the *People's World* because of Steve Murdock's coverage of the CDC. They respected him—the reporters from the *Wall Street Journal*, the Los Angeles *Times* and other places knew and admired his coverage of progressive California politics. Neither the Los Angeles *Times* nor the San Francisco *Chronicle* had anyone as good as Murdock, and everyone knew it.

Many of the other people I met through Dorothy were genuinely admirable. Sam Kushner and John Kykiri (he was Finnish) were *People's World* reporters who had worked for other newspapers, but had become reporters for a communist newspaper because it often was the only paper telling the truth in those days. Both would have been assets to the staff of any metropolitan daily—and in fact they had written for a number of newspapers. Mike Gold was a columnist who had written a classic of the '30s called *Jews Without Money*.

For a while I worked at an organization called the Constitutional Liberties Information Center (CLIC), reporting directly to Dorothy Healey and Reuben Borough. Borough had been the editor of Upton Sinclair's *EPIC News*, which grew out of the author's EPIC campaign (End Poverty in California) at the bottom of the Depression that almost resulted in Sinclair being elected governor of California.

Dorothy wasn't the only communist who deeply impressed me. Another was Herbert Aptheker. He was based in New York, but after reading some of his books on American history, I also got to meet him, for he would regularly go on speaking tours. In those days, Aptheker's books on American colonial and revolutionary history had been revelations for me. I had devoured Aptheker's books, and then attended all his lectures whenever he came to Los Angeles. I got to know the writings of W.E.B. DuBois through Aptheker. When I got the chance to meet my hero, Aptheker arranged with Sidney Finkelstein, the party's musical theoretician, to put me up in his home in Brooklyn. Finkelstein wrote books on music that were quite brilliant. He made his living founding Vanguard Records, as the employee of a boss who knew he had to work for cheap because he was a communist. Finkelstein had exemplary tastes in classical and jazz, and he *was* Vanguard Records for a long time. Almost all the liner notes were his, even when they appeared under different names, which were his pseudonyms. He was also not so overbearing as Aptheker. He used to share a dinner with me of thick black bread and cheese and butter, and then we'd talk all night.

Perhaps the Communist Party was only a detour in my life. In the mid-'60s I had an opportunity to consummate my lifelong love-hate affair with small towns. I went to work on my first newspaper job, in Pismo Beach, population less than 1,000. Pismo Beach was located on the coast, almost exactly halfway between Los Angeles and San Francisco, the only place north of Santa Barbara where the highway touches the Pacific. For a year, I lived and breathed its politics, its ups and downs, since it was my full-time job to know and write about the town. Pismo Beach confirmed Sinclair Lewis for me, although it was possible I came to town knowing who most of the characters were because Lewis had written about them. It did not surprise me that the police chief ran a bordello, and that the Republican assemblyman, a rich Santa Barbara rancher and drunk named Jim Holmes, used to come by the Pismo Beach Elks Lodge, near the pier, where he'd play poker. He always scooped in large napkins of cash from the "boys" who played with him before returning to Sacramento to spend the public purse.

It wasn't until years later, as a political reporter in Los Angeles, that I learned that maybe Holmes *didn't* always win because of his poker skills. Los Angeles County Tax Assessor Phil Watson, for example, used to play poker at the Jonathan Club on Thursday nights, I believe. Again, Watson may not have been as good a poker player as his bagfuls of cash would have indicated.

Sinclair Lewis described Zenith in the '20s, but the truth was that the '60s had a lot in common with the '20s. Both were opulent times followed by hard times. Sinclair Lewis described Babbitt, his sausage finger with a Masonic ring; Lewis was describing small towns of America in the '60s as well. There were certainly local bankers with Masonic rings on fat fingers.

I got deeply involved in the school district board, as had the local John Birch society. The president of the school board, William Troxell, who was an executive with the phone company, used to climb up and down the telephone pole outside my house, presumably bugging the place. He had found out that I had been a "red" in my recently concluded Los Angeles City College days. Tommy Valentine used to come over to my house to play chess with me; he was the reporter from the Santa Maria *Times*. We were on the opposite side of the school fight—he was a political ally of Troxell. He supported the school board as much as I opposed it. The school board was essentially controlled by Troxell, and the local Birchers. They had hired a school district superintendent, Lewis J. Ferrari, who had gotten his Ph.D. from a Spanish university under Franco in 1952. Ferrari and Troxell were not without community opposition. And some of the teachers tried to form a union. The board struck back, and won the day through various kinds of intimidation. One of the union leaders was a lesbian and when they threatened her with exposure, she committed suicide. Shortly after the suicide, when the town reacted negatively to the death of the teacher, suspecting something was rotten, Troxell and company came to the newspaper office where I worked. Troxell held a news conference and made a speech, dutifully recorded by Tommy Valentine, declaring that after an investigation, the Pismo Beach Unified School District had discovered where all the problems in the school district were coming from. Under a banner headline, "Reporter's Red Links Disclosed," Valentine's report in the Santa Maria *Times* said that the Pismo Beach *Times's* reporter, Lionel Rolfe, was a communist, who had been trained in Peking and Moscow at special schools for agents and sent to America to cause trouble in American school districts. Troxell's cause was further advanced by the fact that he arrived at the front of my newspaper office with the San Luis Obispo county sheriff—a fellow Bircher. My boss was panicked. I was fired. A few of the town's powerful citizens, who were also moderate Republicans rather than fascists, came to me and said they would form a committee to fight for my job. They might have been able to get me my job back, because among their ranks were a couple of the biggest advertising accounts my boss had—a supermarket and a drugstore. I appreciated their support, but I declined—Pismo Beach had become too claustrophobic.

As it happened, after years of bouncing around various tabloid newspapers, Tommy Valentine went to work as a columnist for *The Spotlight*, the notorious anti-Semitic, neo-fascist rag put out by Willis Carto's group, The Liberty Lobby. Once or twice in the mid-'80s, after I had become editor of the *Bnai Brith Messenger*, I toyed with the idea of looking Valentine up. Ultimately I could not. I realized the impossibility of being on personal terms again with a man who worked for people who essentially believe I would be a fit subject for genocide.

Ever since that experience, I've never doubted that the fascist mindset has no use for truth. "Trained in Moscow and Peking". Hell, I had gone to public schools in Los Angeles and a couple of military schools, including one that was rather ruling class and very well-connected. I've never made it to Moscow or Peking, even as a tourist, let alone as anyone's trained agent. Valentine knew me well enough to know that this was totally preposterous.

But the effects of the incident took a terrible toll on me personally and financially. Because of Valentine's story and headline, I was blacklisted by the California Newspaper Publishers Association through much of the '60s and '70s. When I got fired off one newspaper, the publisher called me into his office and told me he had just found out about the story in the Santa Maria *Times* from the California Newspaper Publishers Association. He said he was sorry to see me go, that I was the best reporter who had ever come through his doors, but that he had to let me go, and further, I'd never work on a newspaper in California again. He also said that he would deny everything he told me in court if I tried to sue him.

I didn't, in fact, hold another regular newspaper job until 1968, when I went to work for Scott Newhall, the editor of the San Francisco *Chronicle*, who I think hired me just because I might have been something of a subversive. The *Chronicle* was the only major American newspaper to oppose McCarthyism from the beginning, and the first major American paper to oppose the war in Vietnam a generation later—in great part because of Scott. I worked on Newhall's personally owned newspaper, the Newhall *Signal*, at the end of the '60s, and after that worked at the

*Chronicle*, and then came back to Los Angeles in 1971 to write for the old *Los Angeles Free Press*, the first and most important underground newspaper in the country.

The real beginning of my great disillusionment with the Left came with the discovery that not all anti-Semitism came from the Right. I have stayed away from the organized Left for years now, only because I had determined that I would never join up with any group again. My unnerving came from a frank discussion I had with a friend, a mentor, whose couch I slept on when I was in Northern California, especially after I divorced my first wife in the '70s. Dave McQueen was a prominent radio personality in San Francisco at the time (he was the news department of KSAN, then a popular free-form FM radio station). He was the center of a group of Texas cultural outlaws, almost always more of the Left than the Right, who had moved, lock stock and barrel, to San Francisco from Texas. Janis Joplin was among their numbers; one time he tried to hook her up with me, but I rejected the idea because I thought she was kind of ugly. There was nothing Jewish about McQueen—indeed he had been married to an Arab woman, although he assured me that Arab families were just like Jewish families—too much for a good old boy like himself to deal with. I voiced the fears that had been troubling me of late, about my growing suspicion that the entire Left was harboring a disturbing new anti-Semitism that made no sense. Why was it that Zionism, which is after all Jewish people's nationalism, not to be tolerated, and Arab nationalism or black nationalism was kosher? I told McQueen that I was bothered by the fact that Israel was criticized as if there were nothing redeeming about it. Yet it was the Labor Zionists and socialists who founded the modern state of Israel, who created the kibbutzim, one of the most successful of all socialist agricultural institutions in the world. Israel's pioneers were progressive people, fighting for justice—and at that point willing to compromise with the Arabs when the Arabs were not willing to compromise with them.

McQueen surprised me by agreeing that there was a disturbing note of anti-Semitism in the Left, especially the New Left, that perplexed and bothered him as well. McQueen confirmed my worst fears, for I had come to the Left because of my experiences as a Jew. Yet I was not now prepared to endorse the political right, whose creation fascism ultimately is. I still think that democratic socialism is a solution to the monopoly capitalism we have now. It's the only defensible one for me.

Today I am less moved by the stirring books of yesteryear that so formed my being. I suppose that idealism always takes a back seat to a certain cynicism or even religiosity as one grows older. Maybe that is just the inevitable process of age at work. I came to realize that I am of the post-Second World War American generation of radicals, for whom Howard Fast was our Tom Paine, Jack London and Upton Sinclair rolled up in one. In fact it was Fast's *Citizen Paine* that first made me aware of American history—not the history they taught me in elementary school in the '50s, but real history. Making meaning out of the world was my early obsession and I read everything that I could. And like a lot of others, I was very taken with Fast's novel *Spartacus*, which was eventually made into the 1960 movie of the same name.

When I finally got to talk to Fast, it was years later—in the late '80s. Naturally we first talked about Aptheker. Aptheker had told me that Fast had "sold out" over money—that's the real reason he had left the party. He blamed Fast's wife for this. He said the moment his income fell below $250 a week (in the '50s), Fast gave in to the pressure and left the Communist Party. Now, years later, I interviewed Fast and naturally I wanted to tell him my Aptheker story. Obviously he had a different interpretation of the same events.

Fast was also, at this point in his life, a Jewish nationalist—but then a lot of Jews became communists because of anti-Semitism. Fast wrote a book in 1990 called *Being Red*, talking about his experiences as a communist. The American party in the late 1940s still had thousands of Yiddish-speaking workers from the garment industry, the cigar industry, and various others. The Jewish section of the party even had its own newspaper, *Freiheit*. The Jewish section had heard enough even in the late '40s before the Doctors Plot confirmed Stalin's obsessional anti-Semitism. At one point the National Committee of the Communist Party of the United States decided to issue a formal charge of anti-Semitic practices against the Communist Party of the Soviet Union, charging that "the entire leadership of the Communist Party of the Soviet Union was ridden with anti-Semitism." Fast went to Europe, where he met a member of the Soviet's national committee, a writer like himself. The fellow listened to Fast, and blandly informed him that there was no anti-Semitism in the Soviet Union, and that was all there was to it. The matter never became public, but many Jews left the party convinced that there was a strange new kind of anti-Semitism at work in the Workers' Paradise.

Recently I began contemplating my experience with the party in light of nearly everyone's claim that capitalism has vanquished socialism forever. I'm not so convinced. I think that we are only a few years behind the Soviets in terms of a general collapse. The collapse might be, at first, more cultural and political than economic. This country's culture and politics have become so debased, it is hard to think that this is not intertwined with our economic travails as well. The real genius of Huxley's *Brave New World* was that it so well predicted what would happen to the culture—it's happening now in our music, our books and our films. We may be the world's top gladiators at the moment, but that is a dubious recommendation from the country that once produced writers the likes of Mark Twain, Jack London, Sinclair Lewis, Upton Sinclair and John Steinbeck.

There was a lot of pain connected with my experiences with the party. To this day, I suspect that had the U.S. Communist Party really gained enough power to run the society it would have been a disaster. I still believe that some degree of socialism is as necessary as a degree of capitalism is probably necessary to socialism—a genuinely mixed economy is the only thing that makes sense. What's the point of a society unless there's a basic social contract between it and its citizen? But the people I knew in the Communist Party were not the ones to lead the Revolution. I would not have wanted to see the name of socialism so discredited in this country, just as it has been discredited in the Soviet Union and Eastern Europe by communist parties there. That does not, however, validate the opposite, which is fascism.

# Rootless in Utopia, & Liking It

*I* used to think sometimes about moving to Israel. But that's an unreal notion that doesn't really speak to me. For above all, I am a California Jew. And so far, I haven't found a way to take my Inner Sanctum out of California.

❖

In *A Margin of Hope: An Intellectual Autobiography*, Irving Howe tells his story, which is the almost archetypical American-Jewish second-generation tale, and what it seems to end up saying is that being a real American Jew necessarily means being a New York Jew. But as the old song says, it ain't necessarily so.

Howe reveals his attitude perfectly when he describes what he felt when he was forced to live in Palo Alto, a Northern California university town where he complained of "disconsolate evenings." Where, he asked, "are the sidewalks, the pedestrians, the taxis, the crowds?" He spoke of "a grudging surrender to California nature, the starkness of the coast, the rounded hills of the peninsula, the calming grandeur of the redwoods," as well as observing how living in California softens the mind, resulting in a second-rate culture, self-satisfied and self-adoring, and producing only dope dealers, speed racers, transcendental gurus and beat poets.

Mind you, I've been to Israel. I've heard the incredible Israeli klezmer clarinetist Giora Feidman playing his ancient tunes from Safed. I've heard him, ironically, only in Los Angeles, but when I heard these tunes it seemed as if Jerusalem was only a few distant hilltops away.

Klezmer music is not entirely biblical or even Middle Eastern in its derivation, of course. It is also slavic and gypsy.

And that makes it right for me. I am a Diaspora Jew, and in particular a Californian. When I visited Israel the main thing that struck me was how similar it was to California. I felt a strong ancestral pull—and I wondered just how coincidental it was that I am a Diaspora Jew, yet California, the land where I live, looks suspiciously like the land of my ancestors.

Sure, in California I suffer from a feeling of rootlessness, a sense of loss of the original land where my ancestors wrote their history large and plain upon the landscape. But this is true of most Californians—blacks, whites, Jews and Asians. Only the Mexicans, through their Indian ancestors, have a more organic relationship to the land than the rest of us Californians do.

The wandering Jew was the original exile, but now in the 20th century everyone has become an exile, and California is as good an example of this communal isolation as you're going to find anywhere on the globe.

In the California region of the Diaspora, Jews have been an integral part of this great nation-state's story, beginning with the 1849 Gold Rush and culminating in Hollywood. In the Gold Rush years, California was a utopia for the dispossessed, the malcontents, the crazies, the adventurers—and Jews, who had never really had a comfortable home for long anywhere in the world, fit right in.

One of the most famous names on the Western literary frontier was Bret Harte, Samuel Clemens' early mentor, who had Jewish ancestry.

Everyone knows the story of the Bavarian peddler in the Mother Lode who built the Levi Strauss clothing empire from his efforts. Or take the San Francisco *Chronicle*, now the second-largest circulation newspaper in California and the largest in Northern California, which got its start in the Gold Rush. One day in 1865 one of the DeYoung brothers happened to stop by the telegraph office. Because he knew Morse code, his newspaper, the *Dramatic Chronicle*, got the biggest scoop of them all—it was the first newspaper in the west with the story of President Lincoln's assassination. This put the Chronicle on the map.

The DeYoungs were Jews. Their descendants intermarried with French Catholics until today the Theriots and DeYoungs who still own the Chronicle not only don't consider themselves Jews, but belong to a country club where they don't let Jews through the front door. This is the same club that Cap Weinberger, the former Secretary of Defense, belongs to—who had at least one Jewish grandfather, and a psychology that shows he has been trying to avoid that fact all his life.

Over the years, Jews became part of the power structure of California in a way that would not have been possible, except perhaps in Jerusalem.

German Jews had been very prominent in early Los Angeles as well as San Francisco history, when the town was just an outpost pueblo during the Gold Rush. The German Jews ran department stores and owned important banks—but then during the 1880s and 1890s a period of extreme racism and anti-Semitism settled on the town. After the turn of the century, however, a new wave of immigrants from eastern Europe and Russia came onto the scene, and these took over in the new industries of shmatas, Hollywood, and real estate and became more entrenched.

Nigey, who is Greek and Irish and not Jewish, was invited to speak at a meeting of the Tuolumne County Historical Society because she wrote the book *The Sagebrush Bohemian: Mark Twain in California*. Her appearance was part of an effort to save the cabin where Mark Twain is supposed to have lived in the Mother Lode. For her, the trip was almost as much a heartstrings-tugger as my profound experience of going to Jerusalem had been. She was deeply stirred by the Mother Lode. In part this is because both of us have been professionally concerned with California as writers. We both realized that despite her Irish and Greek roots, she feels more for Sonora, the main town of the Mother Lode, than for either of her ancestral homes; and while I probably feel more for Jerusalem than she would for Dublin or Athens, I share the Mother Lode experience intensely.

Thus you can understand why I say, with no offense to Israel, that when I left Tel Aviv (a day before the 1973 war broke out, as it turned out) going home to California via London, I felt as if this were my Aliyah. Aliyah is the Hebrew word for the experience that American and other Jews have when they pick up stakes and move to the Holy Land, to answer that mystical yearning in their souls generated by thousands of years of history and intensified by their Expulsion more than 3,000 years ago. But for me, the intense emotional experience came upon my return to California; not New York, and even London, but Los Angeles.

I talked at some length with Abba Eban, the great Israeli politician and diplomat, about Los Angeles. He, too, admitted to finding Los Angeles attractive simply because of its diversity. California, even more than the rest of the United States, is the land of exiles. California has become the great big beautiful Diaspora, a community within a nation-state, that belongs to everyone and conversely to none of us. California is still too young to have a substantial history, at least compared to the Middle East. After all, Jerusalem is one of the oldest continuous cities on earth because it has been near the crossroads of Asia, Africa, and Europe for some five millennia.

But there's almost a case of parallel universes working here. There is a fabled sleaziness about Los Angeles and San Francisco and Stockton and Sacramento, but it isn't quite of Istanbul, Alexandria or Tangier proportions. Yet a lot of what I saw in Israel had California deja-vu written all over it. The Holy Land and the Promised Land of California were one and the same, in parallel universes. The seaside town of Haifa reminded me of San Francisco, which gave the place a certain comfort, but I now know I will always live in Los Angeles, not Jerusalem or Haifa.

Still, I cannot deny my yearnings for Jerusalem, which puzzles me as well. I am genetically surely as much Russian as Jewish. My ancestors may have originated from Jerusalem before the dispersion, but many were also Tartars—Genghis Khan no doubt rides amongst my genes. I have now come to realize that my early, and I thought inalterable, predilection for rain and cold and fog over sun and smog—in other words, my love of San Francisco over Los Angeles—was the result of my Tartar, Khazar blood. But I now know that I don't want to live through winters in New York, Moscow, Chicago, or London. Indeed, maybe more of my ancestors did come from the Mediterranean than from the frozen steppes. Thus it was appropriate in Israel that the Sea of Galilee reminded me of Lake Elsinore deep in Southern California, and that the vineyards, the orchards and the blue skies of Israel all seemed scenes that could be almost anywhere in California. Somewhere in the mix of these two places is my personal truth.

I mean, am I an American, an Israeli, a Russian, a Mongol or Tartar, an Ashkenazic Jew with more than a touch of the Sephardic? I am all these things and more, I've come to believe. I can make claims to each of the these identities, but it all gets very confusing here in late-20th century Los Angeles where all of us have become so many things it sometimes seems like a tower of Babel in its most multi-cultural moments. My daughter Haila, for example, is Jewish on her father's side, but Nebraska farmer of German-English descent with a good touch of Native American on her mother's side. Why should I think that a bad thing? A lot of Los Angeles Jews are in situations similar to mine, and a lot of other Jews think we're going to Hell in a handbasket.

But in that little room of mine, the mythical room, I contemplate the nearby elementary school where they now teach in more than 70 languages and dialects—in just one school. The Los Angeles school system, where Jews were once the predominant minority, along with blacks, Hispanics and Asians, now has more tongues spoken in it than in New York.

In a way it is really good that this is all so. The tribal identities blossom forth in Los Angeles like the jacaranda trees. It almost works. Here in Los Angeles Jews and Arabs live and sometimes work and play together more or less peacefully, as peacefully, anyway, as the gays and the Hispanics do in my neighborhood.

There were always blacks and Jews in Los Angeles; they were the generic brand minorities. But now there are Thais and Vietnamese and Syrians and Hondurans and El Salvadorans and Lebanese and Israelis and Persians and Turks.

I am comfortable being a Jew, but when a good friend of mine, Irish and Catholic by birth, converted to Judaism it didn't make much sense to me. Being a Jew is not an ideology or a theology or a religion. The religion is at best but a component of being Jewish. I can reject God and his commandments, and still be every bit as much a Jew as someone who clings to them. It happens, in fact, that my own religious inclinations most come out when I'm reading a copy of *The American Humanist*. Believe me, I have read and loved Martin Buber's *Hasidic Tales* and I have gained a certain reputation as a West Coast Jewish journalist, although in fact I was a California writer primarily before I began writing for various Jewish newspapers. It could be said that I tend to both exaggerate the Jewish and the California in myself and in things, and I am guilty happily doing so.

The real heart of the Menuhin story for me, I now realize, was my grandfather Moshe's story and not so much that of Yehudi. Moshe was notorious to much of the organized Jewish community, in part because of his authorship of books such as *The Decadence of Judaism in Our Time*. I know that my grandfather's views came from his own powerful childhood experiences as a refugee, and were suspect in many ways. He could be both cruel and crazy, but he was not a Schneersohn for nothing. He was a bitter, but also a very life-affirming man, whose Zionism came to be expressed for California rather than Israel. There was a lot of truth in the things he had to say.

Is it true that the return to Zion is at heart racist, as he insisted? I am proud to belong to a people who perhaps more than any other have survived millennium upon millennium. Our story, our past, has been documented like none other. There is a comfort in that continuity, dare I say a strength. Our belief, our eternal vigilance in Jerusalem, has made it the eternal Jewish city for all of us. But the truth is other people have been living in Jerusalem for a long time as well, and perhaps we never accommodated that reality in our yearning for Jerusalem.

Like my grandfather, I also wish not to feel apart from the rest of the human race. I would not want to live in an exclusively Jewish world. I like to mix it up. I am Jewish, but I am assimilated as well. I am a California Jew. No doubt it's a particularly Jewish thing—wishing to be the international people who create a synthesis of all the world's culture. The Jewish experience has made Jews an international people, and the Jewish experience hasn't been just a New York experience for a long time.

I know that I do not, and would not, want to live in an exclusively Jewish world. I've seen my cousins in Israel, who couldn't wait to see
London, New York and Los Angeles because they found their own small
land claustrophobic.

But I was excited when I learned that Silver Lake, the section of
Los Angeles I've lived in for decades, was named by a guy named Don
Silver, a mainstay of the Jewish community then.

A successful writer of second-rate screenplays, Nathanael West
was a fixture on Hollywood Boulevard in or near Musso & Frank's Grill.
He was a Jew and a Communist, and a leader of the struggling
Screenwriters Guild. Of course he's remembered today for writing some of
the greatest Hollywood novels, including *Day of the Locust*. And he influenced the Jewish absurdists of the '50s, Philip Roth and Joseph Heller.

It was also in Los Angeles that Thomas Mann wrote a seminal
20th century novel, Doctor Faustus, explaining his country's descent into
the maelstrom of barbarism and Nazism.

Jewishness seems to always be close at hand. When I talked with
actor and political activist Ed Asner on a few different occasions, I told
him he would always be "Lou Grant," the city editor of television fame—
a tough, talented, honest, fair city editor. I had a couple of great editors
along the way, and Asner had the part down so well. One of my mentor-
editors was absolutely WASP—and the other was of Irish revolutionary
stock who had written a biography of the great Irish revolutionary Parnell.
I asked Asner what nationality was Lou Grant? Theoretically Catholic,
Asner explained, adding, however, that he always thought he had the map
of Israel written all over his face.

The man who made the most intriguing comment about Los
Angeles and Jewry was Rabbi Marshall Meyer, who before he was fired
resided briefly at the University of Judaism's Mulholland campus in a high
administrative capacity. Meyer is the great liberation theologist of Judaism
today—he was close to both Buber and Heschel, and he's now in New York
City. He told me that he thinks Los Angeles Jewry in particular should
offer the world's most creative and dynamic leadership to all of World
Jewry, because so many talented Jews were here as a result of this being
the world's entertainment capital. As it happened, this is not what he
found to be the case.

At the core of Jewish existence is the priestly/prophetic dichoto-
my. The split between the right wing and left wing is intense in Jewish life,
with the right claiming descendence from the priestly tradition and the left

claiming as its own the prophetic tradition. Meyer single-handedly created a Jewish religious renaissance at a time of great decline in Latin
American Jewry. But he is probably better known for the role he played
against the brutality of the military regime in Argentina—which
approached the levels of the German Nazis. A long CBS "60 Minutes" seg-
ment followed him around the world because Argentine President Raul
Alfonsin had appointed Meyer, an American citizen, to the National
Commission on the Disappeared.

Meyer was the prophet during his stay in Los Angeles. "Major
elements of the Jewish establishment," he said, "are mediocre, unimagi-
native and turning off the young and unaffiliated. The result is a Judaism
that's been congealed, frozen, paralyzed and emasculated, from a tremendous orthodoxy of thought." He also complained about the Los Angeles
Jewish community having "an edifice complex" meaning that the size of
the edifice is more important than the content. The buildings become
monuments to their donors, whose name are written large on their sides,
whether we're talking schools, temples or hospitals.

He said that too many Los Angeles Jews refused to recognize that
Jews cannot expect support when they cry out about anti-Semitism, and
ignore the plight of others. They cannot ignore the plight of people trying
to escape death squads in Latin America, and then complain if the world
is too quick to forget the Holocaust. "There is a silence in the synagogues
today about those genuinely trying to escape the death camps," he said.

Meyer was particularly appalled upon his arrival in Los Angeles
when a prominent Los Angeles rabbi said in defense of the Jewish terrorists in Israel, that "after all, the terrorists could have killed all the Arabs
they wanted to—instead they merely blew their legs off."

Meyer came to regard himself as bringing a special message and
warning to L.A. Jewry. His message was that if L.A. Jewry doesn't become
aware of the fight against fascism in other parts of the world, the same
thing may happen to L.A. that happened in Buenos Aires, which was a
great sophisticated city until it was destroyed by fascist military rule.

Meyer also warned Los Angeles Jews about living too much in a
Golden Ghetto; the way he saw Judaism, it should not be based on chauvinism.

Rabbi Shlomo Cunin of the Lubavitcher movement whose ruling
Schneersohn clan counts the MaHaRal—the legendary 16th century rabbi

of Prague who created the Golem—among its ancestors, does not know of science. He probably does not know that after World War II, Norbert Weiner, the Massachusetts Institute of Technology mathematician, wrote a seminal work called *God and Golem*, in which he coined the word "cybernetics," the science about the relationship of man and machine that predicted the impact of computers on society we are just beginning to feel now.

But if ever the Lubavitchers were prophetic, today they are priestly. When I had an assignment to write about him some years ago, Cunin's declaration was that he was taking a "grave chance" in allowing me to write about him in a metropolitan newspaper. And he didn't like what I wrote. So he told me that I was "a soul in torment. Our very existence," he said, "threatens who you are." He paused: "There is no doubt you will return. Maybe not next week, or even next year. But you will return."

I resent people who think they have the right lifestyle for everyone. I don't ever want to live in a theocracy where a Cunin decides what I must live and do. It's been a decade, and so far I haven't returned. In just some very practical ways I could never be religious. I hate rules, picky rules, details about silly things and important things side by side. The Lubavitcher live their daily lives by 613 rules that govern every action they take. These regulations cover everything from dress and food to birth and death, sex and mourning, sadness, gladness and ecstasy. "In every aspect, Torah is the guidemap of life," Cunin explained to me—while I thought, Oh God, spare me!

Also, the Middle Ages, the Dark Ages, all those times when the Church reigned supreme, and Jews dressed in black like Chabadniks still do to this day, does not attract or fascinate me. Cunin and all of them look like escapees from the Middle Ages, but if someone is going to leap full force out of the 12th century Cabala from Safed and Girona into the 20th century, they're bound to look a little odd.

Mind you it was interesting to spend a day with Cunin, working in his little room, which in some ways reminded me of my own secret room. He was working out of temporary quarters in a nondescript apartment on Gayley Avenue, after the original building at 747 Gayley had burned down. Cunin worked in the dingiest spot in the place, in the dining area next to the kitchen of a small single apartment. The various employees under Cunin's ever-vigilant eye had spacious, nice enough offices. But not so Cunin's cubbyhole. It was unkempt, with used styrofoam cups strewn about, and here and there a piece of what he had been eating from those styrofoam cups lodged in his beard. The walls of the cubbyhole were in terrible need of paint, and the chandelier above his already old-fashioned desk was yellow and dirty, and only three of its five bulbs worked. The rug was badly, badly spotted.

Yet there was something warm and homey about the place. Right outside the window were numerous trees, and with the sun pouring through they cast an old-world feeling of shadows in sunlight. The effect was heightened by paintings on the wall of Hassids in Brooklyn, or rural scenes in Russia, full of sun and shadow. Cunin's desk faced not a window, but a large portrait of the Lubavitcher Rebbe, who beamed down on Cunin as Cunin cajoled and wheedled various donations from people in sing-song Yiddish and Hebrew and English, telling Talmudic tales, always ending everything with his constant refrain—"To say the least."

We have gone through the 1992 Los Angeles riots now, and the image of Los Angeles becoming like Beirut, a place full of feuding ethnicities, is not without resonance. I'm not so sure, however, that the riots were as much about class as race schisms.

We California Jews are different, significantly so from the way the Irving Howes of this world see us. We are not peripheral. We might be an even more shining archetype when compared to the phenomena of the New York Jews. The paradox: L.A. is the second-largest Jewish community in the world, and the primary character is our ability to assimilate. Is that so bad? I don't think so. I think it's the very ability to assimilate that has allowed the Jewish people to develop such a continuous historical record. Yes, that makes one kind of rootless in Utopia, but what of it?

*Yaltah in 1949*

# Notes on a Lost Past

haven't much liked the '90s, and I was quite dubious about the '80s, and beyond that the '70s as well. After the great fuel crisis of 1973, when the world was hijacked by the international oil cartel, the '60s truly came to an end. The ugly era of Nixonian doubletalk produced the era of Reaganism, which was mild compared to what the Congress of Gingrich in the '90s demanded. I guess the '60s were my best decade.

Yaltah abandoned me in California in the early '60s, and moved first to New York, to marry a man only 10 years older than I, and then to London. She said she would never return to Los Angeles. She broke her vow twice.

My dad said I had an oedipal thing with my mother. But he was also mad at me when I was 16 for taking her side in the argument that destroyed their marriage. She wanted to pursue her music career; he didn't want her to be gone touring the world all the time—or even some of the time.

So my mother divorced my father, attorney and worker's compensation judge Benjamin Lionel Rolfe, convinced she would be happy in London near her brother Yehudi and sister Hephzibah and in a city where people still loved good music. And she did a lot of touring. There was one very brief stop in Los Angeles for a duo-piano concert with her third husband, Joel Ryce. When the plane landed, she got hives. When it took off, the hives disappeared. My mother had a phobia about L.A. To her, Hollywood, which had seduced many of her friends with big pay to play "junk" movie scores, attracted philistines and charlatans. She believed even good people ended up being corrupted by L.A.

But after Hephzbiah died in 1981, she and Joel made a proper visit to Los Angeles—not to give a concert but to visit her son and two granddaughters. Still, when I put her on an airplane to London I knew I might never see her face-to-face again. I knew this as we sat saying our last good-byes. I had hoped that my mother would have been impressed by how much Los Angeles had grown since she had lived here in the '50s. But I also realized that although Los Angeles may have become one of the country's fastest-growing urban areas in the '70s and '80s, this had done nothing for it in terms of classical music. There was probably more good music being made in the '50s in Los Angeles than in the '90s.

Now I have come to realize that my aesthetic values, and to some degree my political values, come from my mother. Perhaps my mother's world of heroic musicians and writers always was something of a fiction. I

**From left, Heather, Yaltah, Nigey and Haila during Yaltah's only visit to Los Angeles**

hoped time had mellowed her; that her sister's death had broken some bond to her love of London. But it was obvious in the few days she spent here it still was an alien place to her.

I haven't been to London since that 1981 visit. One of my daughters, Haila, has visited her grandmother in London. That's a kind of completion, I suppose. But I expect I'll never see my mother again.

Yet she was an influence when she lived here. Yaltah not only appeared over and over again on most of the local concert stages, young musicians wanting recommendations for Fulbright grants to study in Europe were always at her door. Others sought her help in obtaining faculty positions at local music schools. Contemporary composers like Darius Milhaud, Eric Zeisl, George Antheil and Leon Levitch saw her premiere their works here. In those days, not only did great composers like Stravinsky and Mario Castelnuevo-Tedesco live here, but my mother also played chamber music in the homes of cellists Gregor Piatigorsky, Gabor Reijto and Howard Colf, violinists Joseph Szigeti, Eudice Shapiro and Israel Baker; and violist Michael Mann, son of Thomas Mann. There were also chamber music sessions with many of these same people in our home on Pelham Avenue in West Los Angeles  (I remember when the Westside Pavilion shopping mall at Pico and Overland was an empty lot.)

In some ways the musical life of Los Angeles in the '40s and '50s was very rich—but it was also played out in seclusion by people who lived in European enclaves they created. Many had been refugees from the Holocaust. The Los Angeles natives were profoundly uninterested in classical music. In the stifling atmosphere of the '50s, most of this city's denizens were suspicious of "longhairs" who didn't much care for Frank Sinatra. So the musicians who played chamber music in each other's homes did so with the peculiar passion of people fighting for their lives and souls in a hostile environment.

Amazingly during that second visit Yaltah didn't develop hives at once, but I think that Joel was more impressed by L.A. than Yaltah was. That, however, might have been because Brentwood and Beverly Hills would be as good as anywhere for him to have pursued his career as a Jungian psychologist, a career that he adopted after taking a vow never again to touch the keys of a piano. For many years, before she suffered a heart attack, my mother earned a living as a concert pianist in Europe; there was never a way she could have done so here.

When I showed Joel and Yaltah around town, I concentrated on the new skyscrapers, and the multiplicity and diversity that had crept into L.A.'s old neighborhoods. But I avoided drawing my mother's attention to the Music Center, even though it is one of the accouterments Los Angeles wears around its middle-aged neck like a great diamond necklace. What could I say about the Music Center? The Ambassador in Pasadena has better acoustics. For that matter, so did the old Shrine Auditorium, where I heard many great performances. And what could really be said about the plight of serious music in Los Angeles, when some of Yaltah's erstwhile chamber-music-loving friends still made their living not by playing Bach or Bartok but by breezing through Muzak-type scores in Hollywood's still high-paying "music industry" studios? No, some things had not changed in L.A. in the two decades of its rapid growth.

I didn't dare turn on radio station KFAC, which had originally been a passable classical music station. At that point it was packaging three-minute sets of Broadway show tunes between shrill-voiced paeans to Las Vegas gambling emporiums, although it still presumed to call itself a station for serious music lovers. Some time after my mother left, KFAC became a rock station, and KKGO took over the job of classical music purveyor. I told my mother that KUSC was trying, but every time I turned it on, there seemed to be a Schoenberg marathon going on. I didn't dare tell her something else, too, that the Sunday afternoon concerts where she played so regularly at the old county museum in Exposition Park were now held in an auditorium a fraction the size of the old one. The Phil in its opulence can draw a fashionable crowd, but chamber music, which is what real music lovers most enjoy, was something else again. Audiences in Los Angeles go to classical music concerts these days like they go to church—because they think it the thing to do. How could I convince my mother that L.A. loved good music when it was most proud of the fact that it had become the major home of a synthetically produced rock-and-roll music "industry," a phrase that in itself was designed to revolt my mother's sensibilities? Most good musicians in Los Angeles can't make a living playing classical music, so they work, if they're lucky, in the studios, playing music of a decidedly inferior nature. In London, she argued, even though there is real poverty and actual starvation visible on the streets, the English still keep going to concerts. Musicians keep working, playing good music, not just commercial junk. They are not highly paid, but they are getting by as poorly as the rest of the English working class.

I must briefly digress here to talk about being on the horns (& strings) of a dilemma in the '90s that reflects on what had already transpired. It was with a certain amount of glee I listened to some delicious gossip that a violinist friend had picked up while on a recent trip to Finland. He keeps up with gossip from Finland because he lived and performed there for some years.

Did you know that Esa-Pekka Salonen was involved in a scandal with the Helsinki Festival (which he ran) where millions of dollars disappeared without anyone knowing where? he asked.

My ears perked up at this word about the Los Angeles Philharmonic's Nordic-looking musical director.

I once turned down an offer to be the music critic of the old Los Angeles *Herald-Examiner*, after talking to my mother about it.

She said I didn't want to take the job.

"You'll hear so much awful music you'll get to hate music."

I already had encountered some stormy seas after writing a series about the great musicians who lived in Los Angeles right after the

Holocaust—people like Stravinsky, Castle-Nuevo Tedesco, Darius Milhaud and Arnold Schoenberg.

Yaltah used to concertize and tour with Michael Mann, a violist whose father was Thomas Mann, the great German writer whose greatest novel, *Doctor Faustus*, was written about Schoenberg.

Mann was not a musician himself. When he started writing Doctor Faustus, his son, then with the San Francisco Symphony, was his dad's musical advisor on the project.

Mann's book was, to put it mildly, powerful commentary and satire on Schoenberg. The protagonist, a composer named Leverkuhn, like Schoenberg, created a system of atonality based on numerology, and then created music that reflected the descent of Germany into barbarous, primeval fascism, a theme that dominated Mann's work.

I wrote about the experience more than once, and everytime I did, Schoenberg's son, a local municipal judge, would contact the publisher and try to get me fired from whatever publication I was writing for at the time.

My great sin in the series on great composers and the Holocaust was to repeat what all the various significant musicians, many of whom used to regularly gather in my mother's living room, thought. Almost with out exception, they thought Schoenberg a fraud, and worse. Their sentiments were summed up best by Ernest Gold, a Viennese film composer best known for the music to the movie "Exodus," who said Schoenberg's problem was he didn't "know no good tunes" and that's why he had to create a system to compose by.

After 50 years, Schoenberg made it big—in academic circles. Typical audiences can't sit through a performance of his stuff—including me.

Anyway my dilemma was that Esa-Pekka Salonen particularly rubbed me the wrong way. I had heard him on the radio conduct some Brahms, and I actually was angry. It wasn't only that he didn't understand it or feel it, he was simply disinterested. It didn't speak to him, or to his audience.

When I compared him to his predecessor, Mario Giulini, it was particularly bad.

Giulini took the Los Angeles Phil, which despite its overblown reputation is sometimes quite second rate, and performed Beethoven that made me cry it was so incredible.

So the news about Salonen's travails in his native Finland, which hadn't been written about yet outside his native Finland, brought out the worst in me. A fellow journalist, Jeffrey Stalk, and I researched and wrote up the story about the financial irregularities at the Helsinki Festival which was under Salonen's control.

During the course of writing about the incident, I found out that the Helsinki Festival, which for three decades had been dedicated to classical music, now included rock music.

This underscored everything I had felt by Salonen's lackadaisical Brahms.

I knew I didn't like the man. I confess to nicknaming him Fresser Pecker.

Now, I know I part company with many people when I explain my attitude to rock music.

I understand the validity of rock's roots in blues, but that has become a highly tenuous connection. To me, rock is commerce, not music. Anymore than the importance of the science of physics can be compared to hucksters on television selling psychic nostrums, so rock can't be compared to classical music.

I suppose having rock in a classical music festival particularly offends me because rock music has the power of giant multinational recording companies behind it that can package and sell just about anything, whereas classical music survives because man's nature includes the sacred as well as the profane.

The greatest musical creator of the 20th century was not Elvis Presley, but Bela Bartok. Prokofiev and Stravinsky were no slouches, either. Neither was George Gershwin. But Bartok dominates this century the way Bach and Beethoven did previous centuries.

A while after I had written my piece, Salonen was playing Messiaen's Turangalila Symphony written right after World War II. My wife insisted we go hear it. She said I had to give Salonen a chance in person.

The concert opened with Salonen butchering a Stravinsky violin work as badly as he had macerated Brahms. Surprising myself, I felt sadness, not vindication.

But after the intermission, the orchestra came alive; and this most incredible post World War II music filled the auditorium.

I'm not going to use my hypewriter, but it was great.

I was badly shaken and I pondered the matter at length. Salonen is the musical director, and that is too bad. Beethoven, Brahms, Bach, Stravinsky—these guys are the basis of an orchestra's repertoire.

But he acquitted himself incredibly in the case of Messiaen.

Maybe the way out of the dilemma is simple: have two musical directors, one for post-World War II and the other for all the rest of the previous centuries.

❖

As I said, we digressed. I realized the hopelessness of convincing my mother to relocate in L.A. when we paid a visit to Laura Huxley, widow of Aldous, in the early '80s. Laura asked me to bring Yaltah to her large house on top of the Hollywood Hills. Actually my mother hadn't known Laura when she lived in Los Angeles, although Laura was a close friend of both Yehudi and Hephzibah.

We all sat in Laura Huxley's wonderful, high-ceilinged, white-washed Mediterranean villa. Laura was talking about how much she wanted to go home to Italy, if only for a visit. Both Yaltah and Joel nodded approvingly as we drove down the hilltop from her house. "She was very nice," they said, "and still very European," as if that were a crowning glory in Los Angeles.

I had planned the grand finale of my mother's visit to L.A. We would all drive up to the Griffith Park Observatory. I wanted Yaltah to see by night the great sea of lights that Los Angeles had grown up to become. I thought it would be a dramatic way to show how L.A. had finally become a great city.

But when we got to the top and parked and walked around to the front of the planetarium, which usually affords a breath-taking view of L.A., the fog was rolling in. Instead of seeing L.A. as the great Milky Way in the constellation of great cities, everything had become washed out and blurry.

Since my mother left Los Angeles for the last time, it is sad to note that the quality of classical music has been in decline everywhere, not just Los Angeles—even in dear old London things are looking grimmer and grimmer for classical music. Does feeling lousy about this make me a grumpy old fossil? Guess so! I'll accept that change is inevitable, but not all of it is good. It just is.

Besides, I have mellowed. I see and hear things now that hint at a possible renaissance percolating from underground. The other day I heard an incredible violinist, a 16-year-old named Hiliary Hahn, who comes from Amish parents. Despite the increasing stupidity of the mass culture produced in Los Angeles, the human spirit is still there.

*The "Biblical Menuhin Family"—from left, Yehudi, Moshe,*
*Yaltah, Marutha and Hephzibah*

# California Voodoo

*I*n 1997 Lord Yehudi returned to San Francisco to collect an honorary doctorate from San Francisco State College and to officially bury his parents, Moshe and Marutha Menuhin, who had brought him to the City 79 years before.

He also held a family reunion at the Huntington where my brother and some of my cousins showed up. We ate a meal in a private dining room, and reacquainted ourselves with each other. I met Jodi, the delightful daughter of Hephzibah's son Kron, and spoke more than I ever had before with Gerard, Yehudi's elder son, of whom I had once had a thoroughly negative view. I actually found myself liking him this time.

Some old family friends showed up and one woman told me how she used to help my mother put her baby basket under the Steinway when she played. I guess that's how I got my musical education.

Another woman said she was amazed at how accurately I had described Jack Boden when I wrote about him in the San Francisco *Chronicle*.

I've was nursing some bad feelings over how I was written out of the family fortune. At the behest of my grandparents, and no doubt with the encouragement of Boden himself, I was specifically excluded from the will. I wanted to see my living family, but did not want to attend a concert memorializing my grandparents.

For an eternity my 104-year-old grandmother Marutha lived on a hilltop stone mansion in Los Gatos in Northern California. She had set up a living trust at Wells Fargo Bank—the Moshe and Marutha Menuhin Trust Agreement No. 335-102195—with the help of her friend and quite probably her lover, Boden, who lived in nearby Saratoga, an enclave of multimillionaires.

I kept waiting to become more conservative as I got older. Rather the contrary seems to be the case. So I know the conservative "revolutionaries" who have been plaguing the American political scene of late are not new.

As a kid I used to hear Boden's great rants against what Franklin Delano Roosevelt did with his New Deal during the Great Depression of the 1930s.

They were not dissimilar from today's rants.

That damn pap wasn't true in the Days of the Great Depression, when capitalism as a system had simply ceased to function, and it ain't true now. The interests of the people who have and the people who don't

*The author's aunt and uncle, Hephzibah and Yehudi*

have aren't the same. They keep telling me Marxism is dead, and I guess
I'll take their word for it, but class struggle sure isn't. I suppose my knowledge of class struggle was mostly of the armchair kind, but it seemed real
enough to me.

I learned about class struggle from Boden as he sat in  a comfortable chair on the sunny porch of my grandfather's five-acre orchard
and farm at the top of the highest hill in Los Gatos, next door to the
Novitiate. Mostly he would pontificate on the evils of Franklin Delano
Roosevelt, who he said was a man who betrayed his own class. That got
me interested in Roosevelt and the New Deal.

In Jack's world, that was the worst kind of man—Jack had the same sort of scorn for someone who betrayed his own class as Jack London did for scabs. The difference between the two Jacks was their class allegiance. London talked about scabs as having "corkscrew souls" because they betrayed the working class; Boden talked about how the Roosevelts, especially Mrs. Roosevelt, were damn socialists, who were selling out their class to the communist-Democrat unions.

Both of these very class-conscious men were born poor Irishmen. Jack Boden was an ambitious lad who went to work in a bank, then married an heir of Bank of America's Gianinni family. Along the way, he ended up as a vice-president at Wells Fargo Bank, although the Saratoga estate was more the result of the his wife Inez's fortune.

Like Boden, Jack London didn't graduate from college. But London knew the value of education, even though his education had come from reading books at the Oakland library, under the tutelage of city librarian Ina Coolbrith—appropriately enough the same woman who had been involved in a romantic triangle between those two California bohemians, Mark Twain and Bret Harte.

As a teacher of class struggle, Boden had a world view that was most unappealing. He thought that all the things I loved—libraries, universities, books, museums and orchestras—were unnecessary, and maybe even dangerous—certainly for working people, who were not "responsible." While London reveled in the world of science, and philosophy, and saw them as ways to liberate the species, Boden was uncomfortable with them. They seemed at best tangential and at worst hostile to the business of commerce and finance, which is how he measured the world. Nowadays the Gingriches of this world don't say they're against education, but they don't want to have to pay taxes to provide it, and when they do they want to control it so students are spoonfed only their point of view.

My grandfather Moshe, on the other hand, loved Roosevelt as much as Boden hated him. Because my grandfather was an immigrant who had done well for himself in California, he had an immigrant's outsize patriotism. But he said that without Roosevelt, there would have been no capitalism. He believed the introduction of a social contract was what made raw capitalism work.

As a kid in the '50s, I worshipped Adlai Stevenson and went about campaigning for him. When I got to shake Eleanor Roosevelt's hand, it was the most thrilling thing I had ever done. I knew she was the conscience that was the hallmark of the Roosevelt years.

My mistake was trying to argue with Boden; he came to regard me as a dangerous young man. I had just reached puberty, but he saw me as a Bolshevik.

Maybe I was. But even as a kid in the '50s, I found Boden's beliefs the diametric opposite of the values that made sense. And today, when Gingrich and Rush Limbaugh speak, I hear Boden.

As the family banker, Boden was in charge of the family will; I was the only one of eight grandchildren not included in that will. I think he was very instrumental in that, but I should also be thankful I now have no financial incentive to tempt me into thinking like Boden, Gringrich and Limbaugh.

❖

Yehudi was not sympathetic to my plight when I wrote him in London to protest. I asked him to at least discuss the matter with his beloved mother. My grandparents had refused to see me since my early teen years—for crimes having to do with the "ordinariness" of the parents to whom I chose to be born. Still, my grandparents had always gone way out of their way to send me messages that I was going to be equally treated in the will, even if I had done poorly in this matter of parental selection. Naively, I had always believed this—because if there was one thing I believed, it was that my grandmother was a person of her word.

I felt a little trepidation approaching Lord Yehudi about the matter, because after all these years he still makes it seem as if he's too unearthly for such distinctly non-spiritual matters as money. But I was angry and demoralized, not just because of the money (unlike most of my first cousins, I've always had to work for a living), but because as a young child my grandparents had often been entrusted with the task of rearing me and their validation was important to me.

Those early memories at Rancho Yaltah were good ones, even if later in life I learned that their concern for me was somewhat colored by a desire to destroy my parents' marriage. Marutha disliked my father because he was not "cultured" Jewish. (This from a woman who was peasant enough to butcher her own pet goat and serve it up at one particularly memorable dinner I refused to participate in.)

When my family moved from San Francisco to Los Angeles, in part to escape the influence of the elder Menuhins, Marutha sent a gigolo south to seduce my mother, hoping to alienate her affections from my poor suffering father. I don't think the gigolo was succesful in his assignment. Still, like everyone else in the family, I quickly accepted the fact that

Marutha was not just any ordinary grandmother—she was a figure of great significance and power. For one thing, she practiced voodoo—and I'm sure that long ago a special voodoo doll was made for me. When I learned that I had been cut out of the will, I honestly believed—even if on a conscious level I knew better—that this proved I was some sort of evil presence. Else why would my own grandmother practice voodoo on her own grandson? I was amazed at how potent this voodoo was, especially on one such as me, who prides himself on his devotion to rationality and science.

I was even more amazed when I discovered that my grandmother's voodoo was being carried on by none other than her son. In one particular letter, my grandmother's tone was there in Yehudi's letter to me, who advised me that "a person has the right to do with his or her property or money what he or she wishes," which is obvious enough, but that doesn't mean I have to like it or agree with it. Yehudi further added, in a strangely fatalistic but moralistic tone, "Whatever destiny has in store for you—whether it is demoralizing, infuriating, or whether it is a gift from heaven—I hope you will have to wait a long time for it." I correctly took all this to mean he was not going to put in a good word for me with Marutha.

In fairness, I should mention that in 1978 I wrote *The Menuhins: A Family Odyssey*. I wrote it to deal with various ghosts of mine—and it didn't come out like a *Mommy Dearest*, but rather a paean to the Menuhin genius and western Jewish history. It was excerpted in major California newspapers and magazines, and got mostly good reviews, but Yehudi was not entirely pleased by it. It wasn't because I didn't pour adulation on him. I did. He's used to that. The legend of the man is real; he is something very special. But the truth is, even if Yehudi was a prodigy child with great musical and philosophical wisdom, which he truly has been all his life, he still has not become his own man. The reason he was mad at my book was that I did not pour adulation on either Marutha, or his wife, Diana. As a result, he concluded that I suffered from a deficiency of character and class. But his wife, his father and oldest son have penned manuscripts about the family. And Yehudi has his own *Unfinished Journey*. Yehudi's other sister, Hephzibah, used to joke that she too was soon going to join the "writing Menuhins," but instead created Menuhins Anonymous for those family members who had most recently been cast forth from the inner circle.

Later Yehudi and I made up, and had several enjoyable visits when he came through Los Angeles. And everything was fine until Tony Palmer decided to make his documentary in England for Granada

Television entitled "The Menuhins: A Family Portrait", which was reissued on PBS's American Masters in 1991.

Palmer's Menuhins was a two-hour documentary about a dysfunctional family, and was released as a book. Yehudi was so angry at both he tried by legal and financial means to prevent the documentary from being shown or the book from ever being published. He failed. The London *Independent's Sunday Review* ran a piece under the headline, "The Price of Genius: Sir Yehudi Menuhin answers the charge that his fame was bought at the expense of family happiness." The *Evening Standard* rang in with the headline, "Sir Yehudi and the Yaltah disagreement." In the *Independent's* piece, Lynn Barber described Yaltah recalling "how their childhood was sacrificed for the sake of Menuhin's career; how their ambitious mother controlled every minute of their days, made them read their private letters aloud, chose whom they should see and what they should read." Barber quoted Yehudi as further declaring, "Yaltah tells this story about my mother cutting her hair off—she presents it as an act of barbarity. But if you want to know the facts: Yaltah always loved her hair, she would sit in front of the mirror and comb her golden tresses. She still can't be separated from them, even though they now look ridiculous on her rather wizened face." He insisted that Marutha's cutting off the hair was an act of kindness because Yaltah had been experimenting with a curling iron and had ruined her hair. He goes on about my mother, "She feels that she suffered at my mother's hands and that of course creates a resentment. But in fact my mother is one of the most remarkable and wonderful women in the world, selfless to a degree, having given herself completely to her children, and a woman of great pride, integrity, of absolute honesty, a strong and wonderful woman. And never compromising. Now obviously to a mentality which is rather—shall we say?—ordinary, she could seem forbidding, formidable, because people of ordinary size cannot cope with people of extraordinary size. And so Yaltah makes this kind of superficial, stupid accusation. Yaltah was a special case. True, she had a childhood that was suffering. Not that she was denied anything, but she suffered from the fact that she didn't, in my mother's eyes, measure up to Hephzibah and to me. Maybe that's a fact."

All this public unkindness was later replaced by some long letters between brother and sister, but relations never really warmed up. Ironically, Yehudi once apologized to me for how his mother had treated her daughter. And from a musical standpoint, my mother has her defenders, who suggest that in latter years she was the best of the Menuhins musically. It is true that my mother did not give her solo performance with the San Francisco Symphony until she was 10, but in part this was because she was discouraged rather than encouraged, as her brother and sister had been. Yaltah was an unplanned child—she was the result of faulty birth control. This may have poisoned Marutha against Yaltah.

In the Los Angeles where I grew up, Yaltah was regarded by most of the city's musicians as a musician's musician.

Anyway, you can see that Palmer's documentary really stirred things up. I found his book hard going; what I found of most interest in the book was his description of me. He said that Yehudi Menuhin's nephew had written a "well-researched" volume on the family; he didn't give the name of my book, i.e., *The Menuins: A Family Odyssey.* Obviously that would have required some explanation from Mr. Palmer, since the title of his effort was so close to mine. But the documentary was something else again. I initially heard of it when friends began asking me if I had seen it when it was shown on KCET, the Los Angeles public television station. They said I should. When I saw it I saw why. My book was the script.

But I admired Palmer's work. In fact, more than just admiring it, I was profoundly affected by it. I could see why Mr. Palmer won awards for his effort. For example, I knew my grandmother was alive at 101, but I hadn't seen her in a quarter of a century. I was specifically disinvited from doing so—most particularly by Yehudi. So seeing her in the documentary, I saw that she was still the Godmother of us all. At more than 100, she was a little frail, but had all her faculties. And she was as arbitrary and stern and driven by the vision of being a Cherkess, a Tartar, an Italian princess. She changed her identity quite regularly. But she never copped to being the daughter of anything so inelegant as a schocket (a kosher chicken slaughterer).

Palmer portrayed Yehudi's wife, Diana, as a chattering, overbearing bore, by letting her sound like one, which she does at times. He used my mother to provide the narrative that made sense of the saga. Of course it was like my book, because I had derived much of the book from my mother. The end of Palmer's documentary comes when the camera confronts Marutha herself; and if Diana comes across as a domineering crone, Marutha is the ferocious Godmother. The documentary even makes her a little younger than she is—she was born in 1892, but Marutha has always preferred to give out a slightly younger age. By the end of the documentary, you can see that Palmer meant to portray Yehudi as an Oedipal victim—that's probably carrying it a little too far.

Yaltah subsequently told me she had given Palmer a copy of my book the first time he came to interview her. He read it and then came back with his camera crew and asked her questions based on my book. Actually, had he given me a little credit I probably would not have minded. I like credit, and I'm often for sale cheap. Like most writers and even violinists, I'm a relatively simple, egotistical creature.

But one other thing—I have thought a lot about Yehudi's accusation that I have no class. Yehudi is right. I don't have class. He might have been born in New York and emerged as a prodigy violinist out of the pioneer West at the beginning of this century, but his letter showed me what an Edwardian aristocrat he had become. I, on the other hand, was an American—even more, a Californian. I grew up in California coffeehouses and devoured  Californian bohemian writers like Mark Twain, Jack London, John Steinbeck, Upton Sinclair, Sinclair Lewis. No sir, I was an American. And while Yehudi may now be Lord Yehudi, and Lord and Master of the Universe over there in London, I will tell you what I think of monarchy. I think what Mark Twain thought of it. And I know that Yehudi once upon a time read *A Connecticut Yankee in King Arthur's Court* and also was no apologist for  monarchy. Monarchy is a ridiculous concept, even if the monarchs happen to be rare and unusual people—which, of course, they almost never are.

Although Palmer obviously used my book as a jumping off place for his portrait of the family, there were two major dimensions that were not in his book or documentary. The geographic and religious dimensions were missing from his work.

Perhaps the geography was more important than the religious. Moshe brought his young family to Petaluma, across the bay from San Francisco, in 1917.  Here, on California's sunlit shores, they felt they had found deliverance from torn families and crumbling social orders. Suddenly they were in a new land, a magic land, a holy land, if you will. Certainly San Francisco was the catalyst that freed something in these Europeans. The sun was like an all-powerful hand from heaven that could release human souls from their European bondage. Today, San Francisco Bay is only two-thirds its original size. Much of the original bay was filled in so it could be built upon. The buildings that weigh it down now, those cavernous monsters of commerce, had not yet sprouted in such grand profusion. But when Moshe and Marutha arrived at the Oakland train station, they looked cross the bay at the city. San Francisco was a marvelous "island" in the distance, now sunny, now foggy, a paradise that could only reach by ferry.

For Moshe, San Francisco became "the new Jerusalem" he had been looking for. To me, San Francisco has also seemed boorish and gaudy. Yehudi replied to me that its "beauty, color, variety, excitement, freedom, health and elegance" were in its favor. I answered Yehudi that spit-swollen, plank-floored saloons with swinging doors were its beginnings. The spirit of the grand old European castles or even the high-evolved spiritualism of Jewish wise men were then and still are alien to the reality of Baghdad-by-the-Bay. But that was the very reason the Menuhins took to the place so. The open new environment allowed them to revinvent themselves.

Yehudi, in fact, gave all the credit for the creation of exceptional genius in his family not to family history but all the clean air and water and nutritious food of the period. He points out there were a number of violin prodigies in the 1920s in San Francisco. He was merely the first and most famous. There was, for example, Ruggiero Ricci, a son of Italian immigrant parents. He was born two years later than Yehudi and was taught by the same teacher, Louis Persinger. There was also Isaac Stern, born two years after Ricci. One of the better-kept secrets of the Menuhin family was that Yaltah and Marutha personally delivered the promising Stern his first violin. You didn't have to be Jewish in this New Jerusalem, but being Jewish became an integral part of the California experience. It was an alternative to the New York way of being Jewish. It produced different kinds of families, whether they were part of the mercantile world, or the creative arts. The families were more fluid, more assimilated, but certainly they had a great impact on the place around them.

To some extent I blame the influence of California voodoo for the fact that I didn't have a haimischer uncle or grandparents—or even mother. Yehudi once told me, I thought then in jest, that it wasn't easy to be accepted as a Menuhin—that it was a very exclusive club. I think now that he meant that quite literally. I hadn't wanted to think he was being so cruel, because if I am not accepted into the family I was born in, then I am like a man without a country. I am a man without a family, even though physically my family is quite extant.

For exiles from the European experience, California held particular appeal, which is why both Jewish families and individuals flourished so here. But I could see in my uncle's recent letter the same odd coldness that has plagued the whole family. In denying their roots, many Jews, including my own family, poured their newly released energy into new and more creative directions—playing the violin, making movies, following scientific pursuits, and of course making money. Jews who came to the frontier--which California still was well through this century—adopted the same frontier code as everyone else. There was no social contract, even toward your own family. Family members could be cast aside with voodoo curses, or simply made nonexistent, which is what Yehudi and his mother have chosen to do with me. Maybe this was the curse to the other side of the creativity the West allowed Europe's huddled and oppressed masses.

There were no pogroms, there were hardly even gentlemen's agreements, that could keep Jews down in California. That's why a surprising number of the ruling elite of California are, if not Jewish, of Jewish origin, as opposed to the East. That is why my grandparents sought to hide the mystical, cabalistic tradition that their prodigious progeny were explained by. That made the mystery of Yehudi's incredible prodigiousness even more mysterious—yet in a way his parents were right. And so was Yehudi. What was paradise for Jews in exile from Europe? A place where you were rarely cold, where there was always plenty of good, cheap food, and clean air to breathe. California was truly a Zion for Jews, as much as the Holy Land could ever be.

Lord Menuhin and I share genes of the great Cabalists, those folks in Girona, Spain, and elsewhere, who sought to replace the influence of Maimonides and the Greeks with mysticism. Something of that mysticism is at the bottom of his story, I'm sure of that.

But I liked his comment to the San Francisco *Chronicle* upon the occasion of the family reunion.

Explaining that his next stop was in Santa Barbara, where the Nuclear Peace Foundation was going to give him an award, he said: "These are people who are trying to to work for—what else can you call it—a better world. I've always said that my main mission has been to give voice to the voiceless, whether the violin, or a musical score, or children or trees."

We didn't talk much this time, and who knows if I will ever have a long conversation with my uncle again? We had one awkward moment of hugging each other—glanced at each other a few times, but didn't actually connect. He made some motions to me as if we should talk, but he remained surrounded by people.

We didn't talk. I hope that's OK.

# Unnatural Causes

*Youth of delight come hither:*
*And see the opening morn,*
*Image of truth new born.*
*Doubt is fled & clouds of reason.*
*Dark disputes & artful teazing.*
*Folly is an endless maze,*
*Tangled roots perplex her ways,*
*How many have fallen there!*
*They stumble all night over bones of the dead:*
*And feel they know not what but care;*
*And wish to lead others when they should be led.*
*"The Voice of the Ancient Bard"*
from William Blake's *Songs of Experience*

illiam Blake first wrote his *Songs of Innocence*, and then using some of the same titles rewrote the verses later for inclusion in *Songs of Experience*. Innocence was something he obviously believed can only occur at the beginning of life. Innocence invariably must turn into Experience. We rewrite the dreams if not into nightmares, into something far less hopeful, but presumably much wiser.

It's grown difficult to find that solitude where I can make the case for Innocence, even in my Inner Sanctum, these days. I admire people who maintain a lot of their innocence into later life. I'm having a lot of trouble doing so. For Blake, whoever created the fearful symmetry of a tiger's face was an incomprehensible monster. In the world of Innocence, nothing is known of incomprehensible monsters. But they lurk everywhere in the World of Experience.

So let me just tell you one last story from the yellowing clippings of my experience in the Inner Sanctum, here as the last of the Jurassic summers outside my bedroom windows disappears into a new season. Experience must have a component of Innocence, else all is lost.

I wasn't much surprised when I woke up on a Sunday morning—it was November 7, 1982—to read about the apparent execution-style murders of Hollywood holy man George Peters and his business manager Jim

Henneberry in their heavily guarded six-acre compound in Laurel Canyon. It was all over the front pages of both Los Angeles daily newspapers.

The compound was surrounded by fences with coils of barbed wire wrapped all over the fencing. There was a television camera at the front gate. The property had two houses that occupied about two acres of the six-acre estate. Each house had its own swimming pool. The rest of the estate was orchards and untouched brush land.

Henneberry lived in the front house with a woman and a man whose job it was to provide security. Peters lived in the rear house. Although the compound appeared to be heavily guarded, there was a back gate that could only be reached by hiking up a steep hillside. It was usually left unlocked. The killers must have known this, because there were no signs of forced entry.

At first the police indicated that the founder of the Church of Naturalism and his associate had been the victims of a simple burglary, but by midweek they were not dismissing possible drug involvement.

I came to know Peters and Henneberry in 1979 when they were running their church out of an apartment house at Ninth and Mariposa streets in Korea Town. Off and on for three months that year I taped interviews with Peters, heard his version of his life story, and ghostwrote his biography. I received two progress payments, but when I delivered the final draft I got stiffed. I kept the material, and most of what I am writing now is based on what I was told by Peters. (According to the newspapers, the church released Biography No. 2 to the press; I suspect my version was Biography No. 1.)

When I was working with George, the church seemed to be more crash pad than ashram. Mostly, it was a place where Peters and his adherents engaged in their various odd activities (including, I suppose, the 40-day sensory deprivation exercise required of those who wished to join the group). Later, I learned, George Peters and company had moved to a big estate at the top of the Hollywood Hills, on Woodstock Road near Laurel Canyon Blvd. and Mulholland Drive. The church was allegedly "fading away," and Peters had "gone into video." The group was said to be making a movie about cocaine and throwing wild parties.

Peters had been a celebrity in Chicago in the '60s, but the vibes around him weren't so good by the early '80s in Los Angeles. The source of cash for his activities in Korea Town and, no doubt, in the Hollywood Hills, was vague, and as I learned firsthand, sometimes the cash didn't flow at all.

Yet George Peters appeared to lead a costly lifestyle. During the time I had contact with him, he went on a vacation junket to a fancy condominium in Hawaii, ran the church out of the large apartment building in Korea Town, and took innumerable fancy lunches at Mirabelle and Ma Maison.

The only sour note in George's lifestyle was the group's shabby Cadillac (with personalized plates reading A MENTOR). But the car, which would ultimately play a role in Peters' death, was big and comfortable, and did the job required. It hauled Peters around on his errands— which included trips to Griffith Park for long walks and to Dave's Produce on Hillhurst (now, sadly, gone), where Peters would buy meat. Peters refused to eat anything but the finest food. After all, he was the leader of the Church of Naturalism.

The limousine was used by George's killers as their vehicle for a bizarre escape attempt from the Laurel Canyon compound. They apparently knew enough to get into the back through the unlocked gate, but the front gate was still locked. So after the murder they piled into the vehicle and drove several 100 feet down the winding road away from the estate, where they crashed the limousine through the iron gate, knocking it 40 feet down the driveway. Pieces of a large caliber handgun were found scattered in front of the car that the killers just left there before making good the rest of their escape. The handle of the gun was found broken in several pieces.

The neighbors said they were not surprised at what had happened. They suspected drugs were being bought and sold because there was always traffic in and out—in the early morning as well as the evening hours. But if neighbors got to close to the property, security personnel would pop up out of the brush and warn unwanted visitors off. Security was apparently provided by a number of muscular men who could be seen during the day on the property exercising with barbells.

Indeed, the previous year the property had been raided by sheriff's detectives who confiscated cocaine, quaaludes, marijuana and hashish as well as cash. Peters and Henneberry were arrested in that raid, but the charges never stuck because none of the drugs was found in their individual possession.

Although the night of the murders no one heard any shots or the sounds of a car crashing through the gate, gunshots were a common sound emanating from the estate—as were the sounds of rock bands and all night parties. The neighbors assumed there was a lot of target practice going on there as well as the wild parties.

While in most places such colorful antics would seem a little strange, that part of the Hollywood Hills was accustomed to unusual occurrences. A little more than a decade before, five people had been murdered by the Manson 'family' at Sharon Tate's home in Benedict Canyon—about four miles down Mulholland Highway. Even closer in time and space, four people had been bludgeoned to death in a home less than a mile away during the summer. Those were the murders of which pornographic film star John Holmes was acquitted.

Peters was a magnet to people—at least to some people, many of whom loved him a lot, mentally and physically. Nigey thought of him as a would-be Jim Jones. I kind of liked the guy. He was brilliant—and fascinating to talk and listen to. The newspaper stories of his death described him as a "mystery church" leader. Even though he told me a lot about himself, he also remained a puzzle to me. Parts of George's story made sense, but parts seemed only partly told.

Above all else, Peters was a hustler. He never hid that, either. He wasn't a hypocritical religious leader, he enjoyed good living and that was part of his theology. But he also considered himself a messiah, even if it was obvious a lot of what he did to keep his scene together was sleazy and probably crooked. He genuinely loved his good living, even if it sometimes looked as if he were doing it with mirrors. He seemed to have good taste, in a funny way—no nouveau riche trashiness entered his life. He liked to be comfortable and healthy; he was a zealot against white sugar, for instance, a fact which made him seem strangely familiar since crusading against sugar was something I grew up with. To watch him sitting on the sectional bed-sofa that filled half of his large bedroom as he viewed the wall-size television set was to see how much he loved his toys, and his comforts. It was a grand bed, one that could accommodate a dozen people at a time, and probably had.

George was a hedonist. He liked sex. He was not strongly into monogamy. George told me about the time a young man had come to him, bemoaning the fact that his girl friend had been making love with someone else. "Don't worry," George said he said to the youth. "It's nothing to worry about. You know, it doesn't wear out." At the time of our acquaintance, Peters didn't appear to be heavily into drugs himself, although he certainly liked to smoke good dope. What he really liked, and was obsessed by, were the good things in life.

Into his and his church's philosophy, Peters had put a lot of thought—

some genuinely humanistic, it seemed to me. But he also had potentially evil ideas. I believe he considered himself an enlightened human being who wanted to help others. The trouble, the evil, the weirdness entered his philosophy with his belief that he had supernatural powers. Right off the bat I decided the idea didn't really square with the humanistic elements of his philosophy. After knowing him a while, I concluded he had gone over the line, wherever that line should really be.

George claimed he could glow in the dark. He didn't do it for me, but he did tell me the story of how Mr. X once walked into the room where he was meditating, and Peters was "glowing." Later I learned that Peters' witness, Mr. X, would not directly contradict the story; pressed, he would say there had been a bit of "miscommunication." He didn't actually see Peters glow, but believed Peters could do it if he said he could.

About this time I started getting concerned about being Peters' ghostwriter. The more I became familiar with his thinking, the more I found the notion of being his ghost ill-advised, if not plain dangerous. Peters wanted me to undergo one of his sensory deprivation experiences so I would have greater knowledge of what I was writing about. I declined the opportunity. "Thanks but no thanks," I said. "Just talk into the tape recorder, George, and I'll write it up for you."

When Peters ultimately ripped me off for a month's worth of wages, I was angry, but I was also glad to be rid of him. I didn't know anything specifically against him, but it was hard not to sense something wasn't right. I felt he was at once a charlatan and a genius.

When I first met Peters, he told me he used to run a big drug-rescue program in Chicago in the '60s. I was inclined to think this part of his past was all talk, for he had something of a rich-kid braggart about him. I sensed there was money in his background somewhere, but his demeanor could have been carefully cultivated. My reporter's instinct told me that Peters could not always distinguish between fact and fiction. Yet, when I started working with him, he showed me long articles about him from the major Chicago newspapers that seemed to confirm what he was saying.

One of the articles was a long piece from the Chicago *Tribune's* Sunday magazine that told how Peters first hooked up with his mentor, Dr. Walter Alvarez, the famous doctor, author, and syndicated newspaper columnist. It all started when Peters, working then as a TV repairman, went to Dr. Alvarez's home to fix a broken set. Alvarez was impressed by the young man, who displayed—according to the *Tribune* story—an absolutely encyclopedic knowledge of drugs, especially antidotes to LSD. Earlier, in New York, Peters had been a street-drug guru and was prominent enough to rate a write-up in the *Village Voice.*

But in Chicago Peters wasn't just the subject of a single story. He was big stuff. He showed me a whole notebook of clippings about himself. Alvarez and Peters created their drug-rescue mission in 1965, and it lasted for almost six years. The drug in question was LSD, and their methods generated much controversy. Peters was the first to have a drug hotline, for instance, where people on bad LSD trips could call in for help. But most of the trouble revolved, Peters said, around the way he mixed all kinds of people, of different sexes, of different colors, in the same place. Peters claimed that Mayor Richard J. Daley didn't like this "lack of discrimination" and suggested that Peters go to Hollywood, where all the weirdos already were.

In 1971 Peters did just that, bringing his new Church of Naturalism along with him. Peters and his adherents began working with runaway teenagers and, after a while, he claimed to be dealing with 5,000 a month. In Hollywood, the church apparently also worked with COYOTE, the prostitutes' organization. By the end of the '70s, Peters was concentrating his efforts on an organization called GROW, located on La Brea Ave., just off Hollywood Blvd., offering its own brand of "consciousness-raising" techniques. My impression was that most of his "consciousness-raising" was accomplished through copious exchanges of sexual fluids. Hedonism was the message.

Meanwhile, Peters and his followers purchased the apartment building in Korea Town where, he claimed, they were "continuing to evolve by spending time doing enlightenment research in our ashram." The Church of Naturalism had found a home in Los Angeles. And it was as bona fide a church around these parts as the Catholic Church, at least insofar as the Internal Revenue Service was concerned. Very grudgingly, the IRS gave George Peters' Church of Naturalism the status of a nonprofit religion. In fact, after Peters won his case, the IRS took steps to get the rules changed; these days it is much harder for a new form of religion to get tax-exempt status.

One of the tenets of the Church of Naturalism was that the members did not have to disclose their past history; the past was not supposed to be relevant. Nevertheless, Peters told me his life story for inclusion in the book—and it was a humdinger. Since Peters was an enigma in death as well as life, I will pass on what he told me. It must be emphasized that what follows is based on George Peters' words. It was bizarre, yet some of it added up.

Peters would be the first to say—no, he did say—his life was unusual and bizarre. Born in 1939, he was quite the opposite of a guru in his early years. At times, he said, he was an extreme loner. After an "enlightenment experience" at the hands of the CIA, he said, he began to attract followers, and those followers he made into the community that called itself Naturalism, Inc.

I saw enough of Peters to believe that, for all his cynicism, he did visualize himself as a social worker and he did gain a following. Most of them were fringe people, in one way or another; some were just out of jail, others just out of mental institutions. All seemed to need a half-way house in one way or another. Naturalism's motto was: "We help anyone anytime as long as it hurts no other."

Peters told me that his father was one Cyril Gillis Fitzpatrick. A lower-class New York Irishman, he nevertheless went to Fordham Medical School where, according to Peters, he failed his boards. Peters claimed his father then became a New York City cop, going on into Army intelligence in World War II. When an old Army buddy was appointed to the Secret Service, Peters says the buddy got his father a job in the White House; he became a founder of the Central Intelligence Agency.

Cyril Fitzpatrick met his wife-to-be when he was still working as a New York City police detective. His mother, Peters said, not naming her, came from a wealthy banking family. They met by chance. She once took a fur coat in to be cleaned, and someone thought it might have been stolen. Fitzpatrick went to question her, but didn't press the matter, perhaps because she seemed to have good family connections. Two days later, Fitzpatrick was shot by a cat burglar and wound up in a hospital. The young woman came to visit him and not long after that they were married. "Cyril," as Peters put it, "joined the upper class."

After his father's death, Peters said, everything was wrong in his life. Fitzpatrick had been born a Catholic, but died an atheist. His mother had been born Presbyterian, but turned Catholic.

When his mother remarried, Peters said he was unwelcome, even though he had always been told that he would one day inherit $8 million. It was in 1953, the Korean war was on, and to escape he married a young woman who claimed to be French. He was 16, couldn't get work, couldn't even get a Social Security number. But he found a way into the Navy.

After Korea, he held a number of jobs. One of the more unpleasant, he said, was selling insurance in the ghettos of New York City. One of his duties was personally to collect the overdue premiums. Peters still went home to Florida, but not often. His wife and his mother had not hit it off; she claimed his wife was Italian, not French, and had "gangsters" in her family. And when Peters and his first wife began divorce proceedings, Peters said his mother demanded that he sign over to her the rights to his inheritance, apparently to keep his wife from getting anything from him. Said Peters to me: "I can still remember sitting in the kitchen of her house, listening to her proposition. I thought to myself I just couldn't believe that she would ever give the money back, but, on the other hand, I was thinking that people's moms aren't supposed to do things like that. I finally did sign my inheritance over to her, and that was just what she did." His mother died years later, leaving everything to her second husband.

During his divorce proceedings, Peters said the judge took him aside and said his mother had said if he would just come home, she would pay his bills. If Peters didn't agree to this, the judge said he'd throw Peters into the clink. Peters apparently wanted neither. He packed what few belongings he had and lit out for Chicago, a city he did not know.

The '60s were dawning and Peters, aged 21, was on the streets of a strange city, broke and disillusioned. He stayed away from New York, he said, because his father had been a police captain there. If he went to Washington DC, he figured he'd be recognized there too. But in Chicago he said he felt anonymous. He subsisted on Coca-Cola and candy bars. His health was shot. "I was the most friendless person there ever was."

Soon after he managed to get a job repairing television sets, Peters met a stranger named David in a bar. David claimed to be from outer space, and had come to earth to help people—and he had to find the right agents to do this. "I was supposed to be one of those agents," Peters said.

At this point I began to take Peters' story with an extra grain of salt. Paranoid delusions, I figured. But I heard him out. After all, I was being paid to write his story.

Anyway, Peters claimed he ultimately figured out that David was with the CIA and that the CIA was going "to use me as one of their subjects in the MK Ultra program." There were two programs being run then by the CIA's Office of Scientific Investigation (OSI), Peters said, under which hundreds of people were given LSD and amphetamines and observed over a short period. Of the two programs the more comprehensive was called Artichoke, in which the OSI, he alleged, made detailed studies of its victims, using various drugs, and then peeled back layer after layer of the subject's psyche as if it were, well, an artichoke.

At the same time he got to know David, Peters was friendly with a woman he called Kathy. He said he later learned that she had become friendly with him at the instruction of David. Peters told me he dismissed the initial encounter with David as so much bull, but changed his mind when David gave him a powerful drug. He lay down for a noontime nap under the influence of the drug, not realizing his nap lasted for three days. When he returned for work, Peters said his boss was incredulous that his employee thought he had been gone only for lunch. Peters was fired. And he moved in with Kathy—right where the CIA wanted him, Peters claimed.

Peters' yarn got even more convoluted and bizarre. A few days later, he told me, Kathy sent him to a meeting with David, again in a bar. When Peters arrived, David took out a pencil and a sheet of paper. On one side he had notes about Peters; on the other he made notes as they talked. Peters said he was amazed at the information David had about him, for he had been keeping his past a secret. Yet David knew everything about him, Peters said: who his parents were, who his ex-wife was, addresses where Peters had lived, even personal matters about which Peters was ashamed. Peters said he panicked, excused himself to go to the bathroom, and didn't return.

The next day he changed the phone number at Kathy's, yet five minutes after the deed was done, the phone rang. It was David.

Frightened though he was, Peters said he decided he might as well listen to David and to David's proposal. Part of the deal involved David's telling of everything about himself, and Peters said that meant that he continued to insist that he was a visitor from outer space, here to help mankind. Part of the deal was that Peters had to agree to do whatever he was told.

So one of the first instructions was that he had to quit drinking Coca-Cola and eating candy bars. Kathy, under David's influence, began cooking Peters' meals—Peters said this was good for him because, in the process, Kathy read Adelle Davis' works and he was introduced to health foods.

According to Peters' story, David also made him tell all in his version of "Truth or Consequences." Peters had to tell his life story over and over again, and if things didn't mesh in a psychological profile, David would hassle him until he got what he wanted. "As you know," Peters told me, "it's not easy to sit still and objectively tell about your life. You're always trying to draw events in the best possible light." If David figured he was not telling the truth, there was always a consequence. One such consequence, Peters said, was the time he was forced to dye his hair orange, rub black shoe polish on his face, and then go out and snatch purses on Michigan Ave. Then he was forced to return the purses.

A climatic event came when Peters went to a dentist. He remembered starting to count backward after receiving sodium pentothal and a man walking into the room as he did so. When he awoke in a pentothal haze, the man was walking out. Peters said that David later told him he had confessed to a good many things under the drug's influence, and that he might as well tell his life story again—accurately. The big moment came when he said he admitted to Kathy and David about a homosexual affair he had in high school. After telling the story, he said a great feeling of peace came over him. "Indeed," Peters said, "far more than that occurred. Suddenly the confusion of the last five years began to disappear. I found that I could clearly see the conflicts in my life and what had caused them. My life then passed before my eyes and I began to feel myself transcending both space and time. Then I was lonely, more lonely than I had ever imagined one could be."

"I was standing on the seashore and waves were washing over me, growing larger and larger, and as I grabbed at the waves and sand, they became brighter and brighter. An awareness of oneness with everything began to overtake me, and I became one. I was having," Peters said, "a classic enlightenment experience."

Peters claimed that this experience was the Artichoke experiment, and that he had survived because he had come completely clean. Scores of others supposedly didn't. Artichoke subjects were encouraged, according to Peters, to confess absolutely everything about themselves, but most came to something they couldn't face and retreated into madness.

What came next made me wonder whether Peters hadn't retreated into his own kind of madness. He continued, explaining that when people in these experiments—and, by extension, people in a sensory deprivation situation—get to the point of intense loneliness, they get very scared and want to identify and totally participate in the group putting them through the experience. Peters said the idea of Artichoke was to find and develop loyal assassins who couldn't be traced—"Manchurian candidates," so to speak.

But the CIA failed with George Peters. "Under the influence of pentothal," he told me, "instead of identifying with the CIA, I thought I could take over the world. I thought I had the power to do it and I knew I was right. But then I thought of Hitler and remembered that he, too, had thought he was right. So I thought of the sentence, 'I will help anyone at any time as long as it hurts no other.'"

I forgot now if George's killers were ever caught. I think they were. As I vaguely remember, the whole affair turned out to be just another tawdry Hollywood drug revenge tale. I suspect what really did George in was that he went uptown too fast. Perhaps he and his business manager Henneberry tried to stiff someone on some sort of payment, the way they stiffed me—only they were playing in a different and nastier league, with folks who were a lot tougher and meaner at collecting than hapless free-lance writers.

It made me feel kind of sick to think that I had hung around with someone who, perhaps inevitably, ended up getting brutally murdered in such a tawdry fashion.

I sometimes wondered if all the CIA story was simply George's rich imagination, trying to give a gloss to the fact that he really was only a simple con.

But I think not. Obviously he had impressed Dr. Alvarez, who could not have been a simple fool. And you wouldn't think of Alvarez as someone who would have died after having his head bashed in with a handgun handle, and then shot at point blank range. That part of George's life he kept hidden from those he was trying to appeal to intellectually.

George had the manner of a well-born scion. He had the manner of someone trying to save the world. Maybe there were two sides to George, or maybe there wasn't.

But I believed his story when he first told it to me. Much of it seemed to mesh with everything else I knew about the man. If nothing else, it struck me that the program Peters had laid out for his adherents was somehow like the program David had allegedly put Peters through. It all seemed to back up the sinister vibes I picked up from the Hollywood guru; maybe George really was just an oddball do-gooder with a drug-confused past.

Maybe his CIA past was real, and it caught up with him that night at the top of Laurel Canyon. What looked in the papers to be a simple drug slaying may have been a cover-up for something done by our intelligence agencies. Or maybe the murders were simply what they appeared to be, but that didn't mean the CIA stories weren't true.

I know that the mutual friend who introduced me to George when George wanted a ghost writer never wanted to talk about what had happened to his friend. He was genuinely scared to talk. Maybe he knew more than I did and simply wouldn't talk. Maybe he was just scared in the way I was—that someone he had known pretty well turned out to be just another Hollywood drug dealer.

But even a decade later, my friend, who I saw from time to time, wouldn't mention his name. If you brought it up, he'd move on to something else.

George made all of us feel mighty uncomfortable.

# Part I:
# Death from the Desert

I must now admit something I never told anyone before. On Nov. 22, 1963, when John Kennedy made his historic trip to Dallas, I caught every bit of it on the radio. Here was this popular, liberal president, going to Dallas, into the heart of darkest Texas. I was then in my most radical phase—a poor student at City College, full of revolutionary fervor. The need to overthrow an oppressive society seemed absolutely imperative. And because I was a radical, and not just a liberal, I thought that our dashing new president was a cop-out, just as much an instrument of a rotten, imperialist structure as the worst Republican. My first thought when the dry bullet sounds popped off in Dallas was that these were the opening salvoes of the revolution.

In retrospect I'm ashamed that this was my first reaction. But it was.

I was on my way to friends when it happened, and I rushed to get there and be with them. We had all been affected by Camelot, even if Kennedy was only a liberal and not a radical. There's no doubt his presidency was engendering a special mood. Camelot gave us all a sense that America was on the move—that the years of dreary Republican oppression, stupidity and decline were over. Kennedy signified hope, a quality always sorely lacking when Republicans ruled the roost.

My friends had a television, and we stayed glued to the tube. I had felt that optimism of Camelot, although I also militantly subscribed to the belief that capitalism could not be saved by liberal reform, that the whole superstructure needed to be swept away. A dynamic, exciting leader like Kennedy was in a way even worse than one of those dull, mediocre men of the status quo, like, say, a Nixon. We also always told each other that a Nixon was more likely to cause a revolution than a clever, co-opting liberal figure like Kennedy, but all of us were at least secretly glad Kennedy, not Nixon, was in office.

Yet when the announcer said Kennedy had been shot, an exhilarating thought passed through me. The Tyrant was dead. The phony liberal who would lead to no good had been shot. As soon as I thought that, I felt bad that my mind had even entertained such thoughts. Long live the Tyrant!

The John Kennedy assassination was a defining moment for me, and for my generation. Maybe I had not been a fan of Kennedy's because his politics were far right of my own. But we all knew something had gone terribly wrong with the country beginning with that moment in Dallas. And over the years, as a writer and reporter, I dealt directly with the story on several occasions. That made me feel all the closer to the event itself.

Many years later as I curled up on the large bed with my yellowing newspapers that the birds had beaked away on, I pondered—sometimes with a shiver—my closeness to the events.

That's why the Oliver Stone movie about the John F. Kennedy assassination was so personal a thing for me. I came home and reread that issue of the Newhall *Signal* and also a copy of *New Times* Magazine in which I had written pieces about the Robert Kennedy assassination.

During the '60s I spent enough years as a small town police reporter and general assignment reporter to know that the Warren Commission's explanation of how President John F. Kennedy was killed just wasn't believable.

I was an obsessed doubter of the official version almost from the beginning. Obsessed, because like so many people for whom the nickel finally drops about the JFK assassination, I had quickly come to the next inevitable conclusion—if you can kill a president by conspiracy and get away with it, that means you have successfully staged a coup de `etat. And if you have staged a strange kind of silent coup in which you simply take power but don't announce it as such, life goes on but with a lot of unease. Perhaps every president since the Kennedy assassination has been illegitimate.

Stone's movie was about New Orleans District Attorney James Garrison's trial of Clay Shaw, whom he believed was part of the conspiracy to kill Kennedy. One of the reasons I had never believed the shots came from the Book Depository Building was that I had heard an ABC reporter saying without hesitation "The shots are coming from the grassy knoll!" There was no mention of the Book Depository Building in the opposite direction, where the lone crazed assassin Lee Harvey Oswald supposedly did his evil deed.

I had worked with the Garrison people on the Shaw trial because of my involvement with Colonel William Gale, named by Garrison as part of the conspiracy.

On a June evening in 1968 when Robert Kennedy, John's brother, was killed, I sat listening to a man on a couch in the front room of a suburban tract home within easy driving distance from downtown Los Angeles. In six hours it would be midnight. Fifteen minutes after midnight presidential aspirant Robert Kennedy would be gunned down in the Ambassador Hotel near downtown Los Angeles.

The fellow I was interviewing was telling me about how Kennedy was part of the "Jewish-Communist conspiracy." As he talked he was fondling a gun with a mammoth-sized silencer. When he got angry he would brandish the gun, so much that I got quite nervous.

This was Colonel Gale, a former top aide of General Douglas McArthur. Gale later became better known as the Reverend William Gale, co-founder of the anti-Semitic Identity religion, which became the official faith of the Rev. Butler of Hayden Lake, Idaho.

At that time, I didn't know much about Gale. I was just a young reporter interviewing a congressional candidate. He was running against the incumbent Edwin Reinecke, who later became lieutenant governor under Ronald Reagan, and ultimately was the first Republican to go to jail in the Watergate case. When extensively questioned about the matter, Reinecke had admitted to me that he had many nagging doubts about the official version of the Kennedy murder, and so the *Signal* played that up big. Soon enough, the *Signal* was running articles and pictures meant to discredit the Warren Report.

In 1968 Gale was not yet known as the mastermind of the Posse Comitatus. There were rumors of links to paramilitary groups, but mostly he portrayed himself as just another stockbroker working in Glendale who was also an investor in high desert real estate. Nothing was too far out in his initial campaign. He emphasized his military record. He had joined the Army at 16 and at 26 was the youngest lieutenant colonel in the army. He later became one of three officers selected by General McArthur during World War II to direct guerrilla operations in the Philippines. He called himself a "constitutionalist." When asked about a group he had formed called the California Rangers, Gale denied that it was a paramilitary group. He said it was "volunteer civil defense group" comprised of former Army officer friends of his.

A few days before I interviewed Gale, Garrison tied Gale into the Kennedy assassination. Gale's name was linked to a mysterious former KKKer named G. Clinton Wheat, who had served prison time on a murder rap, and was on the run from a Garrison subpoena. When they caught up with Wheat, he had been hiding out in a cabin in the Sierra in Shasta County. (Gale would later move to the same area and run his Posse Comitatus there.) Wheat was supposed to have owned the house at 233 S. Lafayette Park Place near McArthur Park in Los Angeles where Gale and a few others had discussed the conspiracy to kill John Kennedy, according to Garrison. Gale told me that he was an acquaintance of Wheat, but denied everything else, although he did provide me "off the record" a thumbnail sketch of his acquaintance. Later, Garrison executive assistant James Alcock told me that Gale was definitely a very good friend of Wheat.

Not surprisingly, Gale suggested that Jim Garrison was probably an agent of Castro. And with what was obviously meant to be an ironic touch, he allowed to me as to how he personally had liked Kennedy, even if he didn't agree with his politics, and speculated that the assassination "looked like an inside job." Gale attacked Reinecke for having confessed his doubts about the Kennedy assassination to me. "It isn't a congressman's job to investigate things like this. That's why there are organizations like the FBI. If the agencies have investigated it, that's it, unless there's good reason to believe there's hanky panky."

Gale had showed me his shiny new Land Rover, which in a few hours he was going to drive to "the Midwest" to visit relatives he hadn't seen in years if he lost the election to Reinecke—which, of course, he did. He talked a lot about his hero General Edwin Walker, and former Alabama Governor George Wallace, whom he dismissed "as a coward, a politician who would sell out to the niggers."

He complained because his name had been dragged into news stories about Garrison's trial of Clay Shaw for conspiracy "by reporters with Jewish names." I left before the sun sank behind the dry California hills, because I didn't want to stay at the man's house after dark.

And the morning after, I read about how Robert Kennedy had been shot—and remembered vividly Gale and his Land Rover and his gun with a silencer, and thought thoughts too horrible to articulate. A couple of days before I had taken a photo of Kennedy joyously, without much caution, pressing the flesh. My camera lens came within three feet of his face—and I captured a powerful picture that we used in our Robert Kennedy assassination issue at the Newhall *Signal* June 7.

Several years passed. My boss at the *Signal*, Jon Newhall and I went off into different directions—he edited a couple of underground newspapers and college radio station news services during much of the '70s, which often ran news about the latest evidence to emerge on the assassination front. I went more and more into freelance journalism and writing books. In the December 27, 1974, issue of *New Times*, a news weekly then coming out of New York that viewed itself as kind of a left-wing *Time* magazine, Jon and I wrote an article that centered on the attempts by Los Angeles County Coroner Thomas Noguchi and County Supervisor Baxter Ward to reopen the Robert Kennedy assassination of 1968. I used to argue with a friend of mine, Bart Everett, an editor at the Los Angeles *Times*, about whether Robert Kennedy had been the victim of a lone assassin. Bart and his paper believed that. I felt that Noguchi and Ward were onto something when they suggested that Kennedy was not killed by the bullets coming from Sirhan Sirhan's gun in front of him, but rather by   the bullets of someone else who shot Kennedy from the rear. Bart remained convinced by the party line, which maintained that Robert Kennedy was killed by a lone assassin.

About the time that I was writing my *New Times* piece, another assassination movie, "Parallax View," was making the rounds. Friends kept telling me to go see it. It was frightening—in the movie Warren Beatty plays a hard-bitten reporter who gets killed for his efforts to uncover the true story of the assassination of an RFK-type figure. Neither Jon or I were dodging bullets. No one had taken shots at us, nor were the tentacles of a right-wing, quasi-governmental assassination bureau onto us, which was the case with Warren Beatty in the movie.

But during the time I worked on the article, I used to go drink coffee and read the newspaper at Tiny Naylor's at the corner of Laurel Canyon and Ventura Boulevard in Studio City. There I met a man who overheard the conversation I was having with my wife about the story. The man looked seedy, his glasses were scotch-taped, his clothes were shabby, but his talk was big. He regaled us for more than three hours with his incredible exploits in war-time intelligence during the Second World War in the Pacific, and his later exploits with Hollywood producers and Las Vegas gangsters.

He was probably a con man, certainly a salesman. He was selling a machine called a Psychological Stress Evaluator manufactured by the Dektor corporation under contract to the CIA. The machine could supposedly analyze a tape recording and tell if someone was telling the truth or not. The fellow steered me around to the subject of my article, which he had overheard me discussing. He asked if I had sent the story on to *New Times* yet, and for some reason something inside me compelled me to say yes, even though it was still at home in the middle of composition on my desk.

He said we would continue our conversation the next day. I showed up and we talked again, except this time I was more wary, especially as he kept asking me if the story had gotten to the editors yet, and what they had said about it.

I was not too forthcoming with him, and after this I did some research. Indeed there had been a Psychologial Stress Evaluator, which was a fraud that the CIA had financed, and then dropped. Now former CIA agents were making a few bucks selling it where they could. In other words, the PSE was a sort of reward, a franchise, to old CIA operatives. The machine was also being sold to foreign police departments, where it was used to intimidate suspects. I learned that anyone involved with the machine most likely had agency connections—but, in essence, my man, like the others, was just a salesman with a contraption he wanted you to buy or talk about or write about.

It wasn't until years later that I came to believe that Gale knew about what was going to happen that night to Robert Kennedy at the Ambassador. I knew that he knew that I didn't believe him, that I thought that Garrison was onto something with him. In truth, I remember he did not even try very hard to personally convince me of the truth of his alibis. He just mouthed the words that I had to write. He expressed this in his tone of voice and with his body language. In the ensuing years I've come to believe I was kind of lucky to have gotten away from Gale's home with my life.

If Gale were still alive, I would love to have seen Garrison's evidence against him brought into court. But since Gale (and Garrison, for that matter) died half a decade or so ago, that can never be done.

I used to think that surely there were others who are still alive who should be brought to trial.

But as the years have passed, and we move closer and closer to the end of the 20th Century, I'm not so sure of that anymore. After awhile, no one remembers anything.

But that, of course, is not really true. Things are remembered for a very long time, sometimes, and whatever the earthquakes our times passed through after the '60s, we'll be sorting those out well into the next century.

# Part II:
# Death in the Desert

hen my dog Rosie died, she died an enigma. She was a loyal protector. She saved my wife's life early one morning when her old car broke down on a darkened side street, and an angry-looking drunk waving a large crescent wrench approached her, muttering angrily. But he stopped when he saw Rosie. Rosie, who was normally a very gentle dog, rose up on her hind legs and growled and carried on so much that the man dropped his wrench and ran. Rosie was a formidable-looking dog, with shepherd, collie and coyote in her. On another occasion, when a large, menacing man drinking from a jug of wine began threatening Nigey and me on a walk up past the Griffith Park Observatory, Rosie saved both of our lives. Again, the man took one look at Rosie and backed off. Rosie had a lot more of the wild beast in her than a domesticated dog normally had. Her genes included not just those bred from wolves centuries before, but those of an active and perhaps dominant coyote.

Rosie had attached herself to us 11 years before in Griffith Park. She was then a pitiful-looking pup, born of a union between a coyote and a domesticated dog, having a tough time surviving in the "wilds" of Griffith Park, which is one of the world's greatest urban wildernesses.

The familiar, loyal side of Rosie was always very much at home in my bedroom, where she lay at the foot of the bed if she wasn't allowed in the bed. I had tried to train her not to bother the birds, but it was Nick the African Grey who gave her the best lesson in leaving the avians alone. Nick, also known as the Professor, ran up to Rosie's tail, angrily and threateningly repeated "Bye bye," and then gave her a bite on the tail that Rosie never forgot. After that Rosie was pretty scared of these strange feathery creatures that talked like people.

Nick's dominance over Rosie after that was all psychological bluff and bluster, for Rosie would have been quite capable of devouring Nick in a second had she known her own strength.

As the loyal dog in my Inner Sanctum, Rosie was a domesticated creature. But watching her run the coyote trails in Griffith Park, that was the wild side of her.

Rosie always struck me as being somewhat like Buck in Jack

London's *Call of the Wild*—a creature only somewhat happy with domestication.

❖

The mix of wild beasts and terrified humans throws a lot of light on the subject of racism.

Racism is just a variation on the vestigial fear some people carry in them for wild animals—for other species. Racism is the same thing except it is directed not by one species against another but against others within the same species—other homo sapiens.

Some similar kind of primeval thing was operating more than two decades ago when Nigey and I were stuck in a Mojave Desert canyon, the earth  alive with hallucinogenic patterns of stormy, threatening clouds barely passing by the tops of the foothills enclosing us. First it began raining; then it hailed; and finally as we reached the house we were going to, it had begun snowing.

As we walked into the house, Pat Derby raised her tear-streaked face from her arms and stared dully outside. Then she burst into a wail, a woman suffering the grief of death.

"You don't know," she said. "You don't know how it is. He wrestled all his life with wild animals and he dies at the hands of a man with a gun."

She was wailing because a human beast had killed her ex-husband, Ted Derby the lion trainer. The people inside that house were Homo sapiens on a mission to save wild animals from the human beast. And nearby Tehachapi was the home to these murderous Homo sapiens.

Derby was a lion in human clothing. He wasn't a hunter like a lion is, and he wasn't a murderer like some human beasts. The Derbys understood something about that strange tribalism that brings out the savage in human beasts when confronted with wild animals, however.

The Derbys had divorced but they continued together in their cause, saving wild animals from man's brutality. When they finally split from a marriage full of sturm und drang over the animals they lived with, they split up their animals. Pat Derby remained at their compound in Buellton, over on the coast up north of Santa Barbara, managing pretty well. Ted stumbled until he was invited to move to Sand Canyon on the outskirts of Tehachapi.

Pat Derby's tears and wails were not just for Ted, but for his collection of wild beasts, including such "stars" as the famous cougars on the

Lincoln-Mercury car commercials, and television's then even more famous "Clarence the Cross-Eyed Lion." His "trained animals" were much in demand for films and television. But it was always a struggle feeding all the beasts who lived with him, and fending off neighbors who wanted him and his animals out.

People may love seeing wild animals as symbols on television, but confronted with them as neighbors, they became atavistic, and in the case of Ted Derby, so atavistic one of them ended up killing him.

Although Derby was killed by one man, the killer was one among many in the neighborhood who wanted to kill Derby. They knew Derby wasn't one of them. He was more at home with the wild beasts than with the "civilized" Homo sapien.

There are many Sand Canyons in the Mojave. When a man in the Sand Canyon near Tehachapi offered Derby use of his land back of the Monolith cement works, Derby felt he had no choice but to take it. Would he have thought he had a choice if he had known he would be shot to death by Jack Coyne, a nearby Sand Canyon rancher and member of the board of the Tehachapi Unified School District?

I came on the scene four days after the shooting, called there by people concerned about both the safety of the animals and humans connected with them. I had an assignment from the Los Angeles *Times* to write about what was happening. The Derby compound in Sand Canyon was crowded with the "family" of Derby supporters. Joe Agapay, Ted Derby's lawyer and friend, had taken charge. Derby's son, Teddy, then 14, was there with his mother Pat, Derby's first wife. Agapay was telling the group the news—that Kern County District Attorney Al Leddy was not going to file charges against Jack Coyne, that he saw no way to dispute Coyne's claim he had shot in self-defense. Pat Derby could not accept this; she knew Ted. He would never have fired first.

Pat Derby was organizing efforts to take care of the Sand Canyon animals. She heard the lawyer's report, but could not accept the DA's decision. "I hate all these people," she blurted out. "My God, you can't just kill a man and get away with it. These people were so hateful against the animals, yet they allowed someone to kill a man and walk off scot free."

Shirley Keith, Derby's devoted secretary, posed a question: "If the man is out, what are we going to do for protection—how about the girls? They were the only eyewitnesses." Keith was speaking of Shelley Seaman and Julie Rust, the 19-year-old girls who lived at the compound and were apprentices in animal handling.

"The sheriff won't give us any protection if the district attorney can find no reason to press charges," Agapay told her.

Pat Derby looked up. "Where is Coyne?"

"No, no, Pat," Agapay replied. "California law provides for this. When local officials won't prosecute, the state's attorney general can step in. You let me worry about that. You have enough here with the animals."

Joe Agapay was awaiting word from California Attorney General Evelle J. Younger on his plea for intervention in the Derby case, and he was buoyed in his hopes when the Kern County coroner's jury held an inquest and unanimously decided Derby had died "at the hands of another by other than accident." The jury specifically declined to exercise either of its other options—judgments of justifiable homicide or self-defense. Coyne refused to testify at the inquest. But Sandra and Ray Triscari, to whose house Coyne drove right after the shooting, testified. So did Julie Rust and Shelley Seaman and sheriff's deputies Jim Higgins and Ed Bolt, both of whom had been called to Derby's place the night of the shooting.

Leddy said he was still studying the inquest transcript, trying to decide whether the jury's decision and the sheriff's investigation would cause him to change his opinion not to prosecute Coyne. He kept saying that he hoped to make that decision soon.

Agapay's letter to Attorney General Younger had put it succinctly. "If it were self-defense, what was Coyne doing on Derby's property at 12:30 a.m. with a .38-caliber revolver?" Agapay's letter also demanded that a paraffin test or a nuclear fission test be conducted to determine if Derby had even fired a gun that night. Neither Julie Rust, who witnessed the shooting, nor Shelly Seaman nor Nancy Vigrin, Derby's fiancee, both of whom say they heard the argument from inside the house, believed Derby fired a shot. Vigrin, who found Derby's .22-caliber pistol under his body, thought she saw it fall from beneath the bathrobe he was wearing. The last time she saw him through the back window of the bedroom, she said, he had a flashlight in his right hand and a cigarette in his left hand.

Then Younger said that he would leave the matter in the hands of

Kern County authorities entirely. Meaning it was all up to Leddy to do nothing, if he so chose.

❖

Ted and Pat Derby met in a San Francisco nightclub in the mid-'60s. She had a revue act; he sang and played drums in a dance band. He was 6 foot 3 and improbably handsome. They were soon married. What drew them together was their love of animals. A farm boy from upstate New York, Derby had been a movie stuntman and had trained dogs and horses for films. But his best break came when he paid $1 for a lion cub that grew up to be "Clarence The Cross-Eyed Lion" in the long-running television series Daktari. Derby taught his wife everything she knew about animal handling, although her fondness for animals dated from her childhood in her native England.

Early in their marriage they quit music and went to work for movie animal trainer Ralph Helfer on the edge of the Mojave Desert. Then they purchased their own place in nearby Placerita Canyon in Newhall. But neighbors' protests drove them out. These protests—stemming both from fear of the animals and irritation at the noise they made—led the county to rescind permission for them to live there with their animals, and forced the Derbys to move to Buellton, about 150 miles north of Los Angeles.

As time went by, the Derby place became more and more of an animal orphanage, a court of last resort for wild animals who otherwise would have been put to sleep. Most of the animals had tragic histories. Sold as "exotics," many of the bears, lions, wolves, jaguars, lions, Bengal tigers and falcons had been pitifully mistreated. At one point, the Derbys had about 200 of these animals. They tried to support the orphan animals with the "working animals," the trained ones. But even though the Derbys made good money from the movie industry, the food bill was always more than they made and the wolves at the door were of the human kind—creditors.

The Derbys did not use bullwhips and guns to train their animals. Instead they were practitioners of "affection training," and as a result Derby's animals were different. Derby loved to walk into the audience and let people touch and even kiss the animals. Rhoda, the timber wolf, was a favorite with the children. The night before Ted Derby died, he and Pat and Rhoda and her other friends teamed up for a show at the Glendale YWCA; more than 100 children had squealed in delight as they touched and petted the "wild beasts."

Derby also found favor with many filmmakers because his ani-

103

mals were real actors. His nickname was "one-shot Derby"—the footage rarely had to be reshot. On the other hand, he would not permit any use of the animals that he thought cruel. Among his credits was an animal television special with singer John Denver; he also worked numerous times with Bill Burrud, producer of many television shows on wildlife.

Derby took 30 or so animals to the new place at Sand Canyon after the divorce. A landowner had promised him financial backing for a million-dollar animal compound there, where Derby could run an animal training school open to the public.

But the last year of Derby's life proved to be his most troubled. His animals required 400 pounds of meat each week and his debts were piling up; he was bankrupt. His promised financial backing fell through and he didn't have the money to move his animals elsewhere. Meanwhile, the Derby compound in Sand Canyon had become the center of a battle between the canyon's two big landowners. One gave him a $1 a month lease but part of the leased property was owned by another man not sympathetic to Derby's cause. What Derby didn't know was that the fellow who had rented him the land at such a bargain rate was using him to intimidate the adjoining land owner with whom he was warring. The man Derby had signed the lease with was a tough old Kern County landowner with plenty of clout at the county seat in Bakersfield and the capital in Sacramento. The other was a Mafioso type who was later done in by a car bomb in Las Vegas. Derby was caught in the middle of an old-fashioned feud.

And the feud was really only a cover for something far more sinister. Sand Canyon was a claustrophobic canyon, ringed by low-lying barren desert hills that nevertheless gave the feeling of rising high into the sky around the Derby compound. Some of his neighbors may have been involved in a flourishing cocaine trade that used a nearby airstrip for the white stuff coming in from Peru. I learned a lot of the details from a treasury agent who was close to the Derby party of animal lovers.

Other players in the event were some of Derby's scattered neighbors, who owned compact ranching operations, given over in part to the raising of Arabian racing horses. They began worrying about Derby's wild animals eating their equines, and what empathy they had had for Derby when he moved into Sand Canyon quickly diminished as news of his financial predicament got around. As they had in Placerita Canyon, residents of the area complained of the 4 a.m. cacophony created by his 30 beasts.

One of those most incensed was Sandra Triscari, who lived less than 500 feet from the compound. She says that she and her friend Jack

Coyne, who lived four miles down Sand Canyon, as well as others in the canyon, also suspected Ted Derby of rustling cattle to feed his animals. Rustling cattle was enough reason to kill a man in these parts.

It was to her house that Jack Coyne came at 12:30 a.m. one April evening to say that he had just shot Derby in self-defense. Pat Derby had returned to Buellton after the Glendale show, but on learning that Derby had been shot, immediately made the long trip back to the hospital in Bakersfield.

Derby died about 4:30 a.m. She did not get there in time to say good-bye.

Ironically, the animals were not at the Sand Canyon compound when Derby was shot and killed. The Tehachapi Justice Court, at the urging of Derby's neighbors, had ordered the animals removed. Derby had earlier been granted some continuances of that order, but ultimately he had to comply with the orders to avoid going to jail. He sold the animals to Robert Schultz, a film industry entrepreneur and a Derby admirer. The transaction was for $1. For the last few days before Derby's murder, Schultz sheltered the animals in a barn on his secluded ranch just north of Tehachapi, aware that he, like Derby, was in violation of Kern County zoning laws. The animals were to be moved to two permanent sites—the East Bay Zoological Society's zoo in Oakland's Knowland Park and some Indian-owned land near Lone Pine. The Indians reportedly were ready to welcome Derby's animals because they had heard of his gentle ways. Now that Derby was dead, however, neither plan was feasible.

The Knowland Park setup would have been the fulfillment of a lifelong dream for Derby. He wanted a place where people could learn to handle wild animals and he had hoped that filmmakers would come there to learn so that they could produce movies about animals that were more realistic and, more important, not cruel to the animals.

The Sand Canyon compound, situated at the corner of Sand Canyon and Bonanza drives, was a ramshackle place; its 40-year-old structure was the oldest in the usually dry, rocky canyon. Coyne lived four miles down the canyon, near the Monolith offramp of the major highway linking Mojave and Tehachapi. At the bottom of the canyon, where Coyne lived, there was plenty of wide open space for the 16 head of cattle he kept. But up at the Derby compound, the canyon walls were close together and he and his immediate neighbors were physically closer to one another.

Beyond the Derby compound, on Bonanza, Derby's closest neighbors, the Findleys, were very opposed to his animals. About 600 feet up Bonanza was the home of Sandra and Ray Triscari. Directly across the road from Derby's place was Crimson Farms, an Arabian horse breeding operation owned by Tom and Chris Scott. Many of the canyon people were popular musicians who had done well for themselves. One Christmas, for example, Beetle George Harrison had spent three days and nights in the canyon with the Scotts.

The only real canyon original was Coyne, who had worked at the nearby Monolith Cement plant and quarry for 40 years as its chief electrician. It had been 15 years since he had retired, although he still worked on some of its installations.

Later in the day Nigey and I had left the compound and gone into Tehachapi to check the place out. On the lonely road back to the compound, a big cement truck came right up on us and honked and tried to run us off the road. I didn't get a look at the driver, but later I wondered if it had been Coyne himself who had seen our car among the mourners gathered at the compound.

It was entirely appropriate that something sinister would be connected with that cement plant even today. I don't know if a cement plant right in the middle of the desert is in itself sinister, but the place had been born in sinister manipulation that would have made it a perfect set for a scene out of the movie "Chinatown." It had been created at the turn of the century by some of the key figures of the Los Angeles Aqueduct project— General Harrrison Gray Otis, publisher of the Los Angeles *Times* and William Mulholland.

Monolith was built to sell the concrete with which the aqueduct was built 70 years ago. The cement was of inferior quality, but that didn't become apparent until many years later. I did a little calculating—this guy Coyne had been working around the cement quarry for a long time. He knew what bodies—literally—were buried where, no doubt. But he hadn't been around long enough to have been part of the original corruption in which the plant was born. And it did not escape my notice how ironic it was I felt some protection writing about this as a reporter for the Los Angeles *Times*.

Upon our return to the canyon (we outran the cement truck) we talked with Chris Scott, a tall, English-born former Playboy Bunny who made no attempt to hide her distaste for Derby. "He looked haunted," she said, "like a hunted man. I felt sorry for him, but I just wanted him to go, to be out of here. He was too polite at those zoning board hearings; he was always so polite and humble he made me feel uneasy. He was a tall, handsome man, so he shouldn't have been that way. Something was wrong."

Chris thought of the Derby house as spooky and troubled. Once she had tried to find out if there had ever been a murder there. She said that she was hoping to go in with the Findleys to buy the place and tear down the house and build corrals. She bitterly resented the presence of Derby's wild animals because she believed they presented a clear threat to her horses. She felt it was hypocritical of others in the neighborhood to take their children to see the animals, then publicly protest Derby's presence. Chris said that Derby did not take enough safety precautions, that she was constantly afraid one of the animals would get loose and kill her valuable horses.

The night of the shooting she had gone to bed early, so had heard nothing. But she did dream that her car was having a flat tire and suggests this may have been a subconscious registering of the sounds of the shots below.

Sandy Triscari, the unofficial mayor of the Sand Canyon community, had a seemingly charitable view of Ted Derby. "He was very personable, a real gentleman," she said. "I had originally talked the neighbors out of protesting his plans for a million-dollar animal compound. But when he lost his backing and was broke, and kept getting continuance after continuance to keep from moving out of the house, people came to me and said, 'Gee, Sandy, you told us not to protest and look what's happened now.'"

Triscari emphasized in her interview with me that she and her neighbors were not animal haters. Indeed, one of the things that got everyone up in arms against Derby, she said, was the time he killed some horses to feed his animals. He had bought them from a veterinarian who was going to put them to sleep. "He came and apologized, but that wasn't enough," she said. "My children love horses, and it was a terrible experience. We heard him shoot and heard them dying. I told him I couldn't accept his apologies."

Triscari said that while Chris Scott was concerned for her horses, she herself was concerned for the canyon's children, including her own daughter. The school bus picked up the children in front of the Derby compound each morning, and Coyne had protested at a school board meeting that the situation was potentially dangerous. But Coyne's real personal concern, said Triscari, was cattle rustling. "Jack lost lots of cattle to rustlers," she said.

By almost everyone's account, Coyne's obsession was rustling and he frequently patrolled the canyon area and drove out those he did not feel belonged there. One rancher, Bud Hansen, who owned several hundred range cattle in the area, complained that about three years earlier Coyne had pulled a rifle on him over a dispute about the ownership of certain cattle. "Later," said Hansen, "Coyne took shots at me and a guest who was visiting from the East."

By the time Hansen complained to the sheriff's deputies, Coyne had already called them with his side. He said he had just been shooting at coyotes. The deputies told Hansen there wasn't much they could do.

"My visitor packed up and went home. The frontier was too much for him," Hansen said.

Others told of Coyne bragging how he had caught a couple of rustlers and skinned them alive. Triscari insisted that Coyne was "a real nice guy" but most folks thought he was a mean character, quite capable of doing the things he bragged of.

She showed me a packet of photographs of the neighbors, including Coyne. There were pictures, too, of Beetle George Harrison.

Coyne went into seclusion after the shooting, refusing to make statements to anyone. The sheriff's investigators had to rely on Ray and Sandra Triscari for Coyne's version of the shooting. Coyne's phone was disconnected and Sandra Triscari was unable to convince him to talk to me.

Coyne was first held by sheriff's investigators on suspicion of murder, but after three days in jail was released by Leddy. Leddy said sheriff's deputies originally told him Julie Rust, who witnessed the shooting, did not see enough to make a good witness. "So really, there were two witnesses, and one is dead. The other said it was self-defense. What do you expect me to do?" Leddy said.

Derby was standing at the edge of his property and Coyne was in his pickup truck on the county road when the shooting occurred, according to sheriff's investigators. They said the men could have been anywhere between eight  inches to five feet apart. Shootings are not uncommon in Kern County. In 1975 there had been 53 such murders, and most, said Leddy, were the results of domestic quarrels. He added, "Most end up going to trial."

Coyne and Derby met twice that fatal night. Soon after the Derby party returned from the Glendale YWCA show, Coyne showed up with sheriff's deputies Ed Bolt and Mike Whitten. Triscari says she thought she heard "mooing" from the back of the Derby house and called Coyne, thinking it might have been some of his cattle. She says she saw Derby and the girls carrying something into the house in a tarp and thought it might have been a dead cow. But, as it turned out, the "mooing" apparently was only the sounds of the animals still in their cages on Derby's truck.

It was about 10:30 p.m. Derby invited the deputies to look around his property. But he ordered Coyne off the place, saying in front of a sheriff's deputy, "You've caused me enough trouble." Julie Rust, who was with Derby, said Coyne was flashing his flashlight into the cages and upsetting the animals. Derby warned Coyne to stay off his property, elsewise he would have to use his gun. The deputies convinced Coyne to leave.

After completing their search, the deputies went to talk with Coyne at the Triscari house. Triscari said they stayed about a half hour and that Coyne then stayed on until past midnight. She recalled telling Coyne as he was leaving, "Be careful going by Derby's. He'll be hot—you know, the sheriff's deputies finding those wild animals on the property means he'll go to jail for sure. Be careful, Jack."

"Don't worry," Coyne replied. "Derby won't try anything."

A short while later he was back.

"You'd better call the sheriff," Triscari said he told her. "I just shot Derby in self-defense." Triscari said she thought at first he was joking.

Coyne, she said, told her that Derby had come running out of his house and had bounded toward him, waving a flashlight. She said Coyne called out, "I'm Jack Coyne. What do you want?" Coyne told her Derby was shouting a string of profanities and Coyne suddenly realized Derby was holding a gun. According to Triscari, Coyne told her (although he refused to discuss details of the shooting either with sheriff's deputies or through his lawyer) that he had his .38-caliber pistol to his right on the seat of his white Chevy pickup. When he saw Derby had a gun, Coyne told Triscari an unlikely scenario in which he aimed at Derby's chest, hoping just to stop him, not to kill him and, on the second shot, aimed for Derby's face. (The coroner said either shot would have been fatal.) Coyne insisted Derby fired first.

People in the Derby compound told a different version of what happened the morning of April 12, 1976. Around 12:30 a.m. Julie Rust, plagued by bad dreams about dead birds being chopped up and a terrible choking feeling, said she woke up and went to the kitchen for a drink of water. She had been sleeping on the floor in a sleeping bag next to the living room couch on which Shelly Seaman slept. She wanted to sleep near-by because she was scared.

Rust was a shy girl who had been kidnapped as a child. The experience left her wary of people and rather withdrawn, but she was very attached to Derby and the animals, and she was becoming more outgoing. From the kitchen window, she said she saw what she assumed was Coyne's truck. It was old and white like his truck, she said, although she couldn't recognize makes of cars. The truck was going very slowly, with its lights off, on the south side of the building, she said.

Rust ran into Derby's room. She and Vigrin watched Derby searching out back, but then Vigrin, thinking everything was all right, closed the shade. Rust left the bedroom, went out back to meet Derby, and walked down the driveway where she had seen the truck gliding by only a little earlier. "Was it Coyne?" she asked Derby, holding onto the sleeve of his robe.

She said he replied, "It must have been. Maybe he was going up to the Triscari residence because he left something behind."

Then—according to the testimony of all three women in the house that night—Coyne's horn honked. They said that Coyne was calling Derby out. Derby ordered Rust to turn on the porch light and get back inside the house. She begged him not to go to Coyne, but when she saw he was going to, she ran back and took a rifle from the gun rack inside the house. Coyne was still in the truck when she got back to the door and she said all she heard was "a smack," as if Coyne had hit Ted with his fist. Ted jolted and slumped to the ground.

Rust said she told deputies originally she heard only one shot—now, on reflection, maybe two. Derby's closest neighbors, the Findleys, told deputies they heard three.

Rust said Coyne looked down at Derby from the truck and then at her. "I was still holding the rifle. He just stared at me and then drove away slowly."

For a while, Janice Seaman, Shelley's mother, and Shirley Keith were left to care for the animals at Schultz's Tehachapi ranch. Pat Derby had said she could take some of the animals, but not the bigger ones. She had to return to her place in Buellton because she had her own animals to take care of.

Shelly Seaman was an especially enthusiastic apprentice. I first met her mother Janice through Laura Huxley, widow of the great writer Aldous Huxley. Janice had done volunteer work at the Los Angeles Zoo as a youngster, but watching Derby work with animals was even more exciting. "You'd ask him why the animals did this or that, and he'd say it was because the lion thought you were going to do such and such. He knew what the animals were thinking, and once you sat down and thought about it, you realized he was right."

I thought of a brief conversation I had had with Cleveland Amory, the writer who headed up the National Fund for Animals and wrote wonderfully funny novels, when I first got to the compound. Amory had called the Derby compound as soon as he heard the news of the shooting. He told me that "when children watched Derby and his animals, they were watching the communication between Ted and animals as much as either the animals or Ted alone. This very ability," Amory added, "engendered hostility in prejudiced people."

To Derby's coterie of animal lovers, Tehachapi was mean country. One of the popular tales around the compound was a conversation overheard between a chef and a waitress in a coffee shop. "Yeah, honey," the chef said, "we used to shoot niggers and coyotes, but you know, we're damn near out of coyotes now."

The three said Derby would not have shot first if he shot at all, and if he had he would not have missed. "He was an excellent shot," said Vigrin. Also, as the three women tried to comfort Derby while he waited the 45 minutes before the ambulance from Bakersfield and sheriff's deputies came, he kept repeating, over and over again, as if in astonishment, "He shot me. He shot me." Shelley Seaman remembered that "not one goddamn person came to investigate or help" during the time he lay there. Sgt. Burt Pumphrey of the sheriff's homicide detail didn't find this so surprising, "not out there in the middle of the night."

Added Pumphrey, who headed up the investigation, "The physical evidence cannot tell you who shot first, and you have to give the defendant the benefit of the doubt. I think the DA is right—he couldn't have gotten a conviction on the evidence we have."

Pumphrey added he didn't order a paraffin or a nuclear fission test because neither test would be conclusive. He was convinced that Derby did fire, though, because his gun chamber had two expended bullets, and there was a bullet dent on the rim of Coyne's truck door. But no .22-caliber bullets were found on the scene.

Leddy said he had never even heard of Derby until the shooting, despite the fact his deputy in Tehachapi, Gino Spidoni, was prosecuting Derby over the animals.

Janice Seaman made sure the animals were kept alive while looking for a home for them. She felt each animal was a very unusual example of its species. She felt there was a lot these animals could teach our species.

As we near the end of the century, the animals who were at the center of the Derby affair are all dead. It's been enough enough years that most died of natural causes. Seaman and her colleagues spent their personal fortunes and time to save the animals and keep them together. After being moved from one compound to another, the ones that hadn't been dispersed for one reason or another finally ended up in the Wildlife Way Station which is now in Little Tujunga Canyon in the Angeles National Forest. The station has been run for more than a quarter of a century as a rescue and refuge for wild and exotic animals. It is a non-profit organization supported by grants, members and tours.

Seaman said that she knows the battle continued in Tehachapi. Some allies of Coyne died mysteriously in a cafe shoot-out—some have suggested that among the animal lovers were some hombres every bit as mean and tough as Coyne and his kind.

She is hazy about the details of all this, admitting she doesn't want to know any of the details of what happened. She just has private suspicions.

Pat Derby went on with the battle for wild animals—her latest efforts in the '90s reportedly having to do with protecting elephants in a Northern California town.

My story never made the *Times*. I wrote it up, and my editor Beverly Beyette and I spent hours going over every word making sure it could all stand up in court if necessary. At first reading the legal department at the paper agreed it was air tight. The story was scheduled to run in the *Times* and Ted Gunderson, the paper's top photographer then, went out and took some hauntingly beautiful photographs to accompany it. I went away on a trip to San Francisco. On the day the story was due out, I picked up a copy of the paper but the story wasn't there.

I put in a long distance call to Beyette. She told me at the last minute the legal department had killed it—not because there were new real doubts but because Evelle Younger, who was by then the state's attorney general and had a reputation as being entirely beholden to the newspaper, had prevailed upon his many contacts in the legal department not to run it.

She indicated he was protecting people in Kern County who did not want any bad publicity.

The federal agent who had been my source on the story was not surprised that Younger had prevailed on the paper not to run it. He said that Kern County was run like a feudal barony, at the behest of a few of its biggest landowners.

Beyette sounded quite dejected when she told me the story had been killed. Not much later quit her post as editor of the "View" section, although she did go on to write for the paper.

I was scared. Suddenly I felt abandoned. As a writer for the *Times*, I had felt some protection. But I knew Coyne was a killer, and it wasn't until a few months later when he died that I felt relief.

The story ultimately appeared in print, and there never were any legal repercussions because it was indeed an airtight story. The story ran with Gunderson's photos in the old Los Angeles *Free Press*, which was then edited by Michael Parrish. Parrish went on to work at the *Times*— first as the editor of the Los Angeles *Times* magazine and then as a writer in the financial section.

For a while I understand that Truman Capote was interested in the yarn as a result of my story. But Capote died before anything came out of his interest.

Rosie also has died. In her last days we would take her to Griffith Park and one time we watched her bound up the side of a mountain after a full-blooded coyote, perhaps someone she had grown up with there. She ran almost as fast as the coyote but not quite fast enough. For a moment we feared she was going to disappear forever as she bounded over the mountain top after that coyote. But she finally did return, and by the time we got home a violent rain was lashing the windows of our home and Rosie was all settled in at the bottom of our bed.

I remember looking at Rosie, and then at Nick the African Grey. We have a curious relationship with our animals who are not quite wild and not quite domesticated. It's not the same relationship we have with "pets." They are not quite pets, but if we take them from the wild, they "need" us.

We need them as well.

*This photo by Gary McCarthy, showing the author with a stack of his book, In Search of Literary L.A., appeared on the front page of the Los Angeles Independent. In the lower bottom is Rosie the dog. Wuzzy the cockatiel is perched proudly on top of the book the author is holding, and Nick the Arican Grey is on his right shoulder.*

# Dinosaurs in the Bedroom

he fact that birds are descended from dinosaurs is only now becoming understood, with all the implications therein. The notion has been there since the beginning of paleontology. But by the '20s, it had been forgotten, not to be rediscovered until the '80s, with the work of paleontologist Robert Bakker. Perhaps birds make us feel obscure. After all, we are now living in the end of man's dominance of the planet, and it looks like we will reign far fewer years than did the dinosaurs, whose descendants still live among us, older and even wiser than most of us will ever know. Their fragility, the brevity of their lives—and our lives—is a haunting reminder of our intertwined journeys.

When I began writing this book, I lived in a 75-year-old house on a quiet, tree-lined, working class street less than five miles from Los Angeles City Hall with my wife and a number of birds who often times had the run of the place. From here we've both pursued writing, and in the case of Nigey, music careers. We also have run a small publishing company, California Classics Books—which mostly publishes Californiana. I work regularly as a newswire editor, and my wife and I write newspaper columns pretty regularly, but mostly we work out of our house.

We had an Inner Sanctum there that I didn't need to take a train trip to get to. The bedroom was converted from a porch, and the way the sun came through the ivy-covered windows at different times during the day added to the magic of the place. My birds particularly loved it, and on warm summer nights just being with them made me understand their ancestral memories of those long ago balmy nights of the late Jurassic.

These reveries about being in the Jurassic were sometimes spoiled by the urban reality immediately around us. This also affected the sense I had of an Inner Sanctum there, especially the couple of times gangs burned down garages just across the street. It's an awesome sight to wake up to from some pleasant mid-summer night's dream at 2 in the morning and see giant flames shooting up into the air just feet in front of your window. Later, someone firebombed the house next door, to the right of us. It was the second time the house was firebombed. The first time the house's owner killed the guy who had firebombed his place, and went to jail as a result. I was never clear on the details of why or by whom the house was firebombed the first time—and less so the second time. But I heard enough to recognize all the usual suspects—sex, incest, money and power.

Arson is the most unnerving kind of warfare. After the riots and earthquake my pyromaniac neighbors confirmed my suspicion that there was little more civilized about my age dominated by Homo sapiens than there had been in the Jurassic when dinosaurs ruled.

The parrots who slept with us on that summer-porch were our pet dinosaurs. The thought always intrigues me with new angles, new gleanings about the nature of things. Birds' ancestors are descended from dinosaurs, those "terrible lizards" dug up all over the globe in the last hundred years or so. We now know that dinosaurs ruled the planet for 150 million years, and still have a great presence on our planet to this day. Dinosaurs live on as birds. I'm sure that's part of the reason we had birds in our bedroom. It's fun to live with dinosaurs. By being part of a bird flock in our bedroom, Nigey and I sometimes came to think of mammals as Frankenstein monsters as compared to our far more venerable roommates.

In these days of floating values, when the worse is often made to appear the better cause, it is hard to keep up one's belief in humanism and science, as opposed to ignorance and superstition. I thrilled to the demonstrations of these virtues in Mark Twain's *A Connecticut Yankee in King Arthur's Court*. I love the idea of slaying the dragons of ignorance and superstition—which to my mind is what religion is. I have some trouble believing in the perfectibility of humankind these days. In my most honest, private moments, I fear the truth is that as a species we are a young and very stupid kind of beast, bent on some sort of rendezvous with self-destruction. We wrought havoc upon this earth the way my blue-fronted Amazon, Hammy, and my Congo Grey, Nick the Professor would if I left them alone too long in a room without locking their cages.

Perhaps we're always at a crossroads, but this time I think the moment of truth has arrived. We can go backwards in our evolution, or forward. We should go with science and humanism, nowadays so out of style, and a belief in the perfectibility of our kind.

There's a lot of evidence we're going in the opposite direction.

What is obviously the most enchanting thing about birds is the freedom flight affords them. That's why they are so mythical and endure so strongly in our collective unconscious. The great dragons of China, the Loch Ness monster, suggest the existence of dinosaurs as archetypes—and since our culture is relatively recent, the "dragons" have survived even if the gigantic monsters they were based upon long ago became extinct. One can't help but wonder about the last of the giant Moas, 20-foot-tall ostrich-like birds, which became extinct only in the last couple of centuries. By all descriptions, these were quite dinosaur-like. They were killed for food by the natives, and the last of them were slain by Europeans in the conquest of Australia and New Zealand.

There is a serious argument being made by paleontologists, some of whom want to eliminate the avian order and call the birds what in fact they are—a kind of modern dinosaur. So excuse a bit of poetic license when I say watching the Amazon waddles down the hallway conjures up images of T.rex striding purposefully toward you, murder in her blazing red eyes. If she were seven or eight feet tall, you would not want to hang around long enough to make her acquaintance.

I suppose I would have to say that Nick the Professor, the African Grey, is more intelligent than Hammy. But I'm not really sure. Hammy is intuitive and creative; sometimes when she and Nigey start singing, especially jazz, it sounds as if I live in a lunatic music school out of *Alice in Wonderland*. The truth is that Hammy is a great improviser, in bits and pieces. Her problem is that she hasn't a long enough memory to be a consistently good musician, but there is music in her soul. Nick, on the other hand, can figure things out far better than Hammy can, and she certainly strings together words and sentences with much more proficiency than Hammy when she absolutely wants to. When she tries to whistle, you know what she's trying to whistle, but it's not a musical rendition. She has a tin ear.

Birds are also gruff as well as extravagantly affectionate when they want to be. Once I turn off the lights, I don't dare turn them back on, for fear that my cockatiels will deafen me with complaints, telling me off for turning on those bright lights. Remember, birds take light seriously. They are far more phototropic than we. They tend, when in the dark, to switch "off," to go to sleep. The cockatiels, as cute and small as they look, are more like the little flying predator-dinosaurs who were their ancestors than you might imagine. They are constantly beaking; parrots gauge everything, it seems, by eyesight and beaking—their beaks are amazing devices, stronger than any other pincers in nature. Numerous types of dinosaurs had parrot beaks. And sometimes the little guys beak as a way of getting attention, saying, rub our heads, or whatever it is they want. The attention isn't lethal, but it is persistent and effective.

Now you can see why it was a serious matter the day I killed Moses Jake Burby. I was taking a nap when our gray female cockatiel, Burbette, woke me up by nibbling on my toenails and squawking with a strange and terrible tone of terror and hysteria I had never heard before. I woke up slowly. Where was "Mo," Burbette's yellow feathered companion? Normally I awoke from naps with Mo's almost comically wide, symmetrical orange-cheeked face and towering yellow crest glowering down on me, looking rather like a yellow toy soldier, or an outlandish escapee from a punk rock band.

Mo most typically sat right over my head, on the arm of my old reading lamp. When she saw me start to stir, she'd begin beaking the light switch until it rattled and made an annoying racket. Mo applied herself to the switch with complete insistence and didn't stop until I reached up, put her on my shoulder, and kept her there for a while, or rubbed her soft little neck and head.

After living on intimate terms with cockatiels, I can tell you that these little Australian parrots are nothing if not affectionate—even in their wild state, where their affection for and (misplaced) trust of human beings sometimes made them popular snacks for the aborigines. Birds have rich emotional lives, and although their little lives may seem unimportant, it is wonderful to watch them grow, and start to figure things out. They are slow learners—parrots are like human beings as opposed to other animals in that they invest a lot in each of their progeny. You can see their strivings as easily as you can see them in a typical middle-class man and woman and child living in the suburbs. I'm sure you could do bird soap operas, and birds across the world would line up on telephone poles outside human living rooms to watch a soap opera on Mr. and Mrs. Bird. Maybe their lives are insignificant, or ludicrous. It all revolves around breeding, but is human life so different? Birds maintain a lot of decorum. But birds cannot always hide their emotions—as Nigey and I discovered in 1989 when we were driving home from Carson and Virginia cities in Nevada, where she had been doing research on her book, *The Sagebrush Bohemian: Mark Twain in California.* We were driving down the eastern side of the Sierra, not yet having crossed over the Nevada state boundary on our way into California, when we saw a truck driver standing in front of his truck, parked at the side of the road. The driver was looking down at a magpie that he had run over, and its mate, just inches away, was grieving in loud, unmistakable tones that any human being or animal would understand as grief. The driver also looked distraught. Just before we saw this scene, we had been commenting on the flocks of magpies, who despite their grumpy name are beautiful-looking, sleek black birds with vivid white stripes on their wings—close relatives of crows and ravens.

Cockatiels are very social animals who will accept a human being, or even several human beings, into their flock. Nigey and I had been flock-mates with Mo and Burbette for close to three years when the tragedy occurred. Weeks before I had a close encounter with death, from which I recovered in great part because of the presence of the cheerful little Mo who lived at my bedside. I had come to value Mo as a bird who knew she was a bird but also obviously thought of herself as a human being. So on that dark afternoon, the first thing I did on slowly waking up was inch up and look over at the manzanita and eucalyptus playground in front of the cockatiel condo. Mo was not there. An icy hand grabbed my soul; there was something about the sunlight coming in through the half-shuttered, floor-to-ceiling window that was wrong—it had a deep gray, empty quality, casting everything in an anxious mood. I called out Mo's name, still expecting that in a second or two there would be a reply—for there always had been during the last three years she had lived with us. After I had called five or six times, there still was no reply. I jumped out of the bed and now I was terrified because I knew Mo was missing. She might be on the hatrack, or the inside of the closet door, or on the towel rack on the back of the bathroom door. Her latest discovery was the shelf of my wife's jewelry, which she had taken to recently. Perhaps she was there.

But no Mo. No fluttering of wings, no feathered helicopter hovering over me, demanding "Scratch my head." This time, there really was—all the old jokes aside—no mo' Mo. The handsome, rugged little bird whose head looked like a well-groomed walrus, and from the side presented a beautiful Semitic profile, was nowhere to be seen.

Mo was a girl although she looked like a soldier. We always assumed that "Moses" was masculine because of her appearance and behavior, and because her breeder insisted that she was. The only problem was one day Mo began to lay eggs. My bird-loving friend Sharon would say the bird was a "bulldyke." I insisted no, she probably was a tomboy. Mo was attracted to Sharon's vain and highly intelligent, diabolical, lesser sulfur-crested cockatoo male named Reggie, who was three times Mo's size. Mo used to go and press her demands on Reggie by nipping at his tail feathers, although she did so playfully, always ready to fly away if Reggie reacted a little too strongly. When we finally realized that Moses Jake Burby was a girl, her name became Mo, short for Moet, we said.

Whether girl or boy, let me tell you why I loved Mo so. Perhaps it had to do with the fact that my two daughters from my previous marriage, Heather and Haila, were grown and gone. Still, in the three years we had Mo, she never failed to cheer me up. I couldn't watch her for five seconds, whatever she was doing, whether it was looking at herself in the mirror, or insisting on taking every shower or bath with me, without feeling better because of her presence. During the month I lay in bed at County

Hospital, I thought about Mo often and wished her bright yellow little form were there in the hospital fluttering around me. Just thinking about her cheered me up. Nigey gave me daily reports on Mo, who sometimes was called other things depending on the whim. Sometimes Mo was Burby. I realized that Burby, the little yellow "toon" (from cartoon), had touched something deeper in my human soul than I had ever known existed. We had acquired Mo shortly after seeing the movie "Roger Rabbit"—and when we got Mo we realized that Mo was a toon, cheerful and poignant, sad and life-affirming. I suppose as a kid I wished I could be friends with a bird, and of course go flying with a bird. When I was 14, I used to listen to Wagner and wish I could fly right into the clouds. Yes, birds are magical. But I never imagined I would have one who would love me as sweetly as did this little creature.

Mo was the perfect helicopter, flying up silently behind you and landing on your shoulder, or buzzing up to the ceiling fan and demanding that she be pushed—she used the fan as a merry-go-round. If you didn't get her hints and give the fan a push, she would fly down to your head, land there, and then return to the fan, showing you what she wanted. Until people get to know and love birds, they believe the old expression "bird brain." Believe me, there are smart bird brains.

Burbette, for instance, owed her life to Mo. One day we left Burbette unguarded for a second while the bathroom sink was filling up with hot water. Burbette, not being as cognizant of the physical world as Mo, went jumping into the hot water and started flapping and drowning. Mo began immediately shrieking and hollering. Nigey came running, and pulled Burbette out of the scalding water only seconds after she had leaped in.

We still thought that Mo was a male when Burbette began sitting on her eggs. But we were bothered because she would chase Mo out of the cage where she had made her nest. We had read that male cockatiels share the egg-sitting duties with the female pretty evenly. Mo was curious about the eggs but Burbette still chased Mo away. Mo would always come back, looking at the eggs, trying to sit on them, and doing so rather clumsily. Finally Burbette got angry. She went up to the bell on the "front porch" of the cage that we had purchased for Mo and Burbette, and although neither Burbette nor Mo had shown the least inclination to use the bell before, Burbette began clanging it angrily with her beak and flapping her wings. She was a ferocious sight, and she literally kept Mo out of the cage so that we had to set up her water and food elsewhere, since Mo wasn't allowed into her own cage anymore.

It was rather comical, Burbette playing the bell the way Scots used their ferocious bagpipes to frighten off their enemies. Mo would invariably go running when she clanged the bell and flapped her wings. And I laughed and said, "Mo, you know this is just psychological warfare. There's no real reason you have to go away just because she's ringing the reverse door bell." I'm sure that Mo was not intelligent enough to understand what I was saying, but damn if a day later she didn't do exactly what I had suggested to her. When Burbette began clanging the bell to drive her away, she merely turned her back and refused to be driven out. Burbette kept clanging—Mo just stood her ground. After a few more such occasions, Burbette gave up on her weapon.

Now, though, I glanced back at the bed where I had just been lying. I cannot describe what I felt at what I saw. My heart was in my mouth. Mo was lying there, not moving. Indeed, she had been crushed underneath me. I could tell that at a glance and couldn't look again. I had killed Mo. I jumped up and ran into the front room, crying out to Nigey. I was hysterical. "I killed Mo," I said. I was shaking; I couldn't move. Life drained away from me. I couldn't pick up the body. Nigey did that; Mo was irrevocably dead, but the body was still warm. I asked Nigey to bury her. She went over to the yard in back of Sharon's house and planted a gravestone, and a neighbor of Sharon's contributed a small juniper tree.

At first I stayed behind because I couldn't bear to see Mo's beautiful body so dead, the life gone. But after Nigey left with Mo's body, I suddenly felt horribly alone. I hurried on over to Sharon's, and saw Sharon and Nigey digging the grave. It was a cloudy gray afternoon and I wept and wept and wept.

I went through several days of intense mourning. I looked up into the sky and saw birds flying free, swooping and playing and chasing, and I burst into tears again for my beautiful Mo. Several days after the burial I walked past Sharon's house and I thought I heard Mo. I saw a bird flying, and for a wonderful moment I cried out because I thought Mo was returning. For a moment I really believed that Mo was back from the dead, but quickly I realized that Mo would never return. I wept again.

Nigey said perhaps it had been Mo's spirit that came flying up. Sharon said that I must not blame myself for what happened, that Mo wouldn't have blamed me; she loved me so. Mo was jealously monogamous with me, and had even bitten Sharon once when she was trying to pet her.

Once I would have been embarrassed to have used words like spirit and soul when talking about a human being, let alone a bird. But Mo had a soul. I guess birds are, to use Jung's term, an archetype. My wife and

I have begun to see birds everywhere—they are everywhere; there are somewhere in the neighborhood of 14,000 species of avians. They are in every people's art, in every people's legends. They are in all cultures, symbols of transcendence.

I guess that smart little parrots like Mo are not typical birds. Mo was a revelation for me. Because of Mo, I began to look at lots of different parrots, and to read about parrots. I became fascinated by parrots and ravens because they are the most intelligent of birds. The way they accepted Nigey and I into their flock amazed me. They would wait until we came home to start eating. They would peep excitedly when we returned from the day's hunt.

So Mo acquainted us with birds that were intelligent—frankly quite a bit more intelligent, I felt, than either the cat or dog. Parrots generally are thought to have the intelligence and emotional life of a three-year-old human child; the difference, of course, is that parrots don't develop much past three, whereas human beings, hopefully, keep developing. Many amazing stories and even laboratory studies about parrots have suggested that as we are destroying their native habitats, which are often in the rain forests, we are destroying animals of surprising intelligence.

I know the story of the famous chimpanzee, for example, who was said to have the equivalent of a 500-word vocabulary. There also have been studies of African Greys, who are known to talk with vocabularies of upwards of a few hundred words—and they use those words with grammar, with syntax, and even with poetry upon occasion. Their conversations are somewhat rambling, but they do address matters, at times, with surprising style and wit. And in one well-documented case, an African Grey has actually read words from cards.

We had continuing discussions about what makes the "burbs," the "little people," or "peeps," so human. They are not human, of course, and wouldn't have the charm they do have if they were. Paul Bowles, in *Their Heads are Green*, says that "It fascinates us to see a small, feather-covered creature with a ludicrous, senile face speaking a human language—so much, indeed, that the more simple-minded of us tend to take seriously the idea suggested by our subconscious: that a parrot really is a person (in disguise, of course), but capable of human thought and feeling." He then describes Indian servants he had in Central America and Mexico who obviously regarded parrots as people.

He gives examples of women working in kitchens who converse all day with their parrots, as if they were really in a conversation when it is their own monologue they are listening to. But the parrot's ability to speak in our language with some facility, enough at least to say hello and good-bye, is impressive. Certainly our dog Rosie, a large coyote-German-shepherd-collie mix, was quite terrified when she met Nick for the first time. Nick moved menacingly toward her, began yelling and screaming like a human being, and then bit her tail, all the time yelling, "Bye Bye! Bye Bye!" Rosie has been totally bamboozled by the Professor ever since. Both our big parrots, unless they are feeling particularly ornery, will walk into their cages, which we will then lock up when we have to go out. They know that as long as one of us is home, they will never be locked up. But when we go, they must be in their cages, for their protection and ours. So I tell them that I have to go—usually "I have to go to work now," and they will stop whatever they are doing (usually sitting atop their cages), and get into their cages, and patiently wait for one of us to close their doors. Nick the Professor repeats after me on the way out, "Have to go to work now" while Hammy utters a piteous "bye-bye" especially if she's sorry to see us going. Upon our return home, the cockatiels greet our arrival excitedly with wild peeping, triggered by the sound of the approaching car engine, which they can distinguish from others. The big guys say "Hi!" I did not set out to teach them these "tricks"—it's just a way we've developed of living together successfully. Parrots like to please their human roommates, but at the same time they can be arbitrarily nippy, because they are in fact wild animals. They adapt nicely to a warm, loving environment where they are dotingly taken care of. But parrots will always be more companions than pets.

When we first brought Nick home, she said nothing for two weeks, and then one day Nigey walked into the bedroom with a doughnut. Nick said, "Have you got some more cookie?" quite insistently. Nigey quickly realized that the Professor could be mollified with a piece of doughnut. We also both learned that when the Professor was asking for a "cookie" you could tell by her tone of voice if she could be satisfied with a cracker, a piece of bread, or a rub of the head. All these things meant "cookie" to Nick. In fact her "I want a cookie," or "have you got some more cookie," or just "cookie, cookie" could become quite annoying. One day she was being insistent with me and I was ignoring her, doing something else. She kept asking for a "cookie," and becoming all more insistent and annoyed with each new utterance. Still I kept ignoring her—I was trying to get something read. Then I heard her say, "Come here, bring your Nick a cookie." I stopped reading. I realized that Nick had just completed a genuine sentence, one that wasn't badly constructed, either. Alex, the famed African Grey who has been used in lots of laboratory studies, who has been written about in the New York *Times* and portrayed on television documentaries, has demonstrated not only an ability to distinguish letters of the alphabet and names of colors, he can also read their names from cards. He also has considerable syntactical ability. Nick, too, had demonstrated that directly to me, so I agreed. "Yes, Nick, for that you get a cookie." And I got up and went to the kitchen to get my Nick a cookie. She had me well trained.

Parrots also have much more developed senses of humor than dogs and cats, who in fact have little; parrots are often eccentric, and quite mischievous when they choose to be, yet they also have a strong and attractive innocence. Nigey suggests that there really is a lot of the quality of Mozart in the birds' voices, with a childlike purity that pulls at the heartstrings so much it is a painful experience. We have heard some incredibly haunting love melodies from cockatiels in their mating rituals, even though cockatiels are not particularly musical birds. The song is not human, it is avian, but it is still as beautiful as Mozart.

I think the biggest revelation was that I felt closer to the birds than I ever had to cats and dgos. Their wings are limbs for another medium. Their wings are not just forepaws. Birds stand erect just like we do. They even sleep erect. And like human beings, they are flock animals. You tend to greet them in crowds, even though birds of the raven and the parrot clans have very strong and distinct individual personalities.

Perhaps my cockatiels numbered among their ancestors the fearsome Tyrannosaurus rex. Many dinosaurs walked and ran erect, were warm-blooded, unlike their lizard reptilian ancestors, and lived and reared their young in flocks. Some enjoyed complex communication skills with their companions—two scientists I know have studied ravens and dolphins in completely different places and times, and both were enchanted by the realization that dolphins and ravens use a system of sounds for communication that rivals and surpasses the complexity of homo sapiens in terms of vocabulary.

Not long ago James Gurney wrote a fanciful story and drew some marvelous pictures for a book called *Dinotopia*, a place where human beings, who have dominated the earth for maybe a million years or so, lived on equal terms with the dinosaurs, who reigned over the planet for an unprecedented 150 million years. It's a lovely story, and maybe not so implausible as at first it might appear. No Humanotopia is as believable as Dinotopia. I don't know for a fact, but I would bet that Gurney knows his birds well, and got to thinking up such a charming place as Dinotopia because he enjoyed his birds. Perhaps he read Robert Bakker, the paleontologist who has singlehandedly promoted the notion of birds as dinosaurs into near acceptance today; an old idea, incidentally, that was originally proclaimed in the last century by Thomas Huxley, but then forgotten until the 1980s.

Nigey and I met Bakker, and he told us about the African Grey he used to work with at the Brooklyn Zoo. He said he thought African Grey birds the most intelligent animal on the planet, save ourselves. He thought African Greys were more intelligent than chimpanzees, orangutans, dolphins—the whole lot of them.

At this writing Nigey and I have six birds. Four cockatiels—Bubba, a white-faced hybrid with subdued gray for contrast, a strutting male if ever there was one, who probably carries a gunrack in the back of his pickup truck; Wuzzy (who replaced Mo); Girlie (whose original name, Burbette, was changed after Moses Jake Burby died); and Cutie, one of Wuzzy and Bubba's progeny (all of them but Girlie make up the Biblical family Peep)—as well as Nick and Hammy. Sometimes Sharon brings over Reggie and his galpal Rosie (Rosie is a giant, rather bald, Moluccan cockatoo)—then we have eight birds in our bedroom. Sometimes Nigey talks about just having to have a parrotlet or two, and then she fell in love with rose-breasted cockatoos, and now what she said would never happen has happened. She wants a matched set of hyacinth macaws.

Surely, this is dementia, this thing I have with birds. But maybe it is only a sort of madness. So one little yellow dinosaur became important in saving my life. I used to live with the mythic bluebird of happiness; now I live with the yellow bird of salvation.

I'd just as soon save the spotted owl as give timber mills another 10 years to finish destroying what they haven't yet destroyed—all of the old forests on the North American continent.

# A Building of Life, Not Death

o amount of riches can compete with the gift of life when death is the alternative. People who are rich can buy better medical care, I guess, but at a certain point they still suffer, they still die.

That's why the most civilizing of places in a modern society are its public hospitals, where anyone can expect to be treated whatever the size of their pocketbook.

At the end of the Dark Ages and the dawn of the Renaissance, the City-State of Venice was run by a Council of Three. No one knew who they were, but the three were probably justified in being as paranoid as they were. The three were feared, and hated.

The Bridge of Sighs was one way—you couldn't go back once you were summoned to it. Across the bridge was a dungeon, and death. No one ever walked across the Bridge of Sighs and survived. Those who took the walk were notified by the placing of their name on a piece of paper in the mouth of the lion at the entrance to the Bridge of Sighs.

Probably many of those whose names were placed in the mouth of the lion were political enemies of the Council of Three, even if the Council of Three was anonymous. Some of those had no real reason to be chosen for death, whether rich or poor.

I contrast this with a public hospital, where the battle always is for life and not death. Sometimes there is such a thing as human progress.

The other day I was looking for something in the bottom of my closet, and came across a picture of myself looking kind of shaky, standing on the steps of the old Los Angeles County Hospital (properly known as Los Angeles County-USC Medical Center). The photograph was on the cover of the old Los Angeles *Reader* in 1989, when I wrote about the 30 days I had spent in the hospital after my wife was told I had a one in four chance of pulling through..

I owe my life to that place, and now they've been talking about replacing it, which made me furious. After the Northridge Earthquake of 1994, the county was able to keep using the proud old structure built in the '20s while the more modern structures surrounding the main building were the ones that actually collapsed. On the walls on the first floor of the big main hospital historic photos document how the place—which actually was not completed until the Great Depression—was built. Maybe there are some things they didn't know about earthquake resistance at the time, but the hospital was so overbuilt with steel and concrete, it was obviously meant to survive just about anything. This, after all, was conceived as the one place in the city which would survive most any calamity, and provide for the needs of the people. They said the old building needed lots of work to bring it up to code, but then, it had needed lots of work before the earthquake. As a patient who spent a month there at the height of a summer, I can personally attest the building needed air-conditioning, for example.

County Hospital was built at  time when people still saw public services such as police, fire, and health, and even education and libraries, as heroic endeavors. It may be that a modern structure would be more efficient, but I bet they won't keep the lobby where a proclamation is engraved in its tiled, concrete portals, promising that no matter how poor a citizen is, in this place medicine is given according to need, not wealth. The proclamation states an obvious part of any social contract a civilized society must have. But nowadays you'd be lucky to get even the Hippocratic Oath engraved on a public hospital.

County officials even talked about the abandonment of most health services in Los Angeles County, plunging us back into the Dark Ages when disease and mayhem destroyed great cities. Now they're planning to build a much smaller hospital, and will farm out the overflow to other hospitals, none of which bodes well for the future of County Hospital. I'm told even Calcutta has a public hospital; but in Los Angeles we may not.

Perhaps you haven't really lived until you've almost died. There is no greater gift a society can confer upon a citizen—a valiant effort to give him or her the health needed to enjoy the blessings of life, whether rich or poor.

Many times during my stay there, I felt I would never get to go home and contemplate in my Inner Sanctum again. During those 30 days, memories of the Inner Sanctum began to trickle out. It took some time for the Inner Sanctum to appear in my life again after spending a month so close to death.

Whenever I had reason to drive down the San Bernardino Freeway east of downtown, I'd pass the Los Angeles County Hospital and my heart would fill with with a clammy fear. Now the fear has been replaced in great part by a lot of other, complex emotions.

Growing up in Los Angeles, that great stone monolith, rising above the freeway with its three stern towers, used to give me much the same feelings of horror as old, dreary, Dickensian workhouses I saw in England. The very sight of that monolith conjured up an a "house of death" image. I had always thought that if you were unlucky enough to have to go there, you'd never emerge alive.

But I now realize that however strong this image of a death house was, it was not based on fact. I had heard stories of friends who had gone in for immediate treatment for what seemed like important emergencies— who had been kept waiting for eight and ten hours before a harried doctor saw them. I had on one occasion gone to County Hospital and seen the patients in hospital beds in the hallways, and watched an old man shuffling along in his hospital gown, open in the back, searching the hall ashtrays for cigarette butts.

County Hospital is the hospital of last resort, and as a free-lance writer then with not much of an income and no health insurance, that was where Nigey took me when I developed chills and a high fever and my genitals suddenly swelled up to twice their regular size. The first doctor who saw me was anxious to dismiss me as a malingerer. My wife insisted on another opinion. The second doctor took one look, and with a grave expression, quickly called surgery. Dr. Daniel Jacobs, the doctor from surgery, put me on a stretcher, told me that I was in a fight for my life, and the next thing I knew I was being prepared to go under the knife.

I didn't remember seeing Nigey until I woke up in intensive care, where I stayed for several days. I did not know until later what my wife had gone through. The initial operation took seven hours. After it was over, Dr. Jacobs admitted to her that when they had begun operating, they had given me a one in four chance of pulling through. Gangrene had spread dangerously close to some very vital regions—the cause appeared to be a case of undiagnosed diabetes. But I did pull through. I had determined that this was not yet my time to die, not at 46 years of age. So I was not surprised when I woke up in intensive care feeling horrendous, but definitely alive.

Nigey spent much of the seven hours with Karen Kaye, a friend who had been married to a doctor who interned at San Francisco General Hospital; she knew about the 36-hour shifts, the intensity of the idealism in her former husband at that point of his life. When Karen visited me shortly after the operation she enjoyed watching the bustle at County, for it reminded her of those early days as a young doctor's wife.

Teaching hospitals are different from most other hospitals. The doctors, usually in their last year of residency, operate in teams. Everything that is done to a patient is discussed and debated, sometimes even in front of the patient; the medical professor is often a part of that team. This kind of medicine has its advantages over the normal situation, where your doctor operates with almost no peer review. He is the king, and what he says goes. If your doctor is particularly brilliant, that can be good. But few doctors are that brilliant; second, and even third and fourth opinions make sense in matters of life and death. So you can make a good case for saying that the medicine practiced at County is often superior, even to a high-rep hospital like Cedars-Sinai—at least for the kind of ailment I had.

I think the thing that surprised me, right from the start, was how concerned nearly everyone who took care of me was. I had had other hospital experiences—a couple of decades ago I spent nearly three weeks in traction in a San Joaquin Valley hospital after being involved in an automobile accident. And in 1985, I went to Cedars-Sinai Hospital for a painful but probably not so dangerous operation for anal fissures. Although at the time I was editor of the *Bnai Brith Messenger*, the pioneer Jewish newspaper in Los Angeles that was approaching the century mark, they almost wouldn't let me into Cedars—despite the fact that a 100 years ago Cedars started as a Jewish charity home for tubercular patients in a house that still stands today on Carroll Avenue in Angelino Heights.

Cedars insisted on $1,000 from me up front, and the Jewish Free Loan didn't deem me a good enough candidate to loan me that money. Actually, I don't carry that much pocket change around and it is hard for me to get hold of that much cash. My usual trauma is, like many people's, how do I pay my rent this month. Others prevailed on the hospital, arguing that after all, I was the editor of the city's oldest Jewish newspaper and it would look bad if Cedars didn't take me. I was in considerable pain. At County they may hassle you for money later, but they take you whether you have money or not.

Furthermore, I can now say that the nurses and doctors at County seemed more genuinely concerned about me than did the staff at Cedars, even if at Cedars I didn't have to sleep in a ward with ten other people— including drunks, illegals and gunshot gang members. I was immediately immersed in a blare of daytime television, full of advertising for cheap insurance, lawyers and soap—mixed with cops-and-robbers dramas and entertainment shows mostly concerned with the war between the sexes. A stay in County Hospital is an immersion in urban reality. There are no phones beside the patients' beds, although there are pay phones down the hall—which is where patients able to get out of bed often stay and kibb-itz. Few patients at County have cell phones.

After I was sufficiently recovered from the original operation, I went back under the knife for reconstructive surgery. For a month, County Hospital was my home. If I didn't get to like it, I got to appreciate it. Most of the nurses were impressively conscientious about their work, and often went beyond the call of duty. When I was in pain, they were concerned. Not just because of medical reasons, but because no one likes to see a human being in pain. You get very attached to people who have that kind of concern for you.

My most vivid memories came shortly after I was shifted to a reg-ular ward from intensive care. Undoubtedly the dream-like memories that stuck with me early on in the visit were influenced by the fact that I was getting morphine shots for my pain—the pain was still intense and the mor-phine was essential. But morphine is, of course, a very powerful opiate, and it is known to produce a peculiar dreamlike state. I got to know my ward late at night and early in the morning swimming in a morphine haze. The ward was green, a favorite hospital color in the '30s; a trend that would still be prevalent except that after a few decades, people began associating that particular shade of green with hospitals, and hence pain and suffering. So more modern designs use other colors. County is not modern. The ceilings are high, the plaster on the walls is real, the light coming out of the old-fashioned fixtures is minimal. It's hard to read in the hospital: it's easier to watch television. The scenic oil paintings that someone placed on the walls years ago, to cheer the patients up, look faded and dreary.

This was definitely L.A., but it's not Westside L.A. Rather, it is the forgotten L.A. of another time and place—substantial, serviceable and solid, in a day and age and place when most things are not. There should have been big fans hanging from the ceiling; the evenings were hot were stifling hot, although the high green walls stayed cool. Small table fans here and there labored to keep the place comfortable.

As the sun set, the breezes were still warm; the moody lighting only faintly lit up the huge room. One must understand something about County—it is a seriously under-funded hospital. At Cedars, for instance, the IV drips are run by computers. At County, it's all done manually. The head nurse one night told me that her greatest fear was messing up on get-ting the right drug flowing at the right time—if she makes a mistake, the patient can die.

At night, the spacious green walls and ancient dusty windows were like a stage setting. In intensive care the pain is intense but you are usually so doped up that even though you can feel it, you are quickly off to sleep. But those first nights when I moved out of intensive care into the tenth floor surgical recovery ward, the foremost thing on my mind was minimizing the pain I felt every time they changed my dressing. There was one nurse, a man who was too rough on me, and showed, I thought, too odd an interest in the whole area of my wounds. I almost felt as if I were rough trade out of a William Burroughs book. I complained about him after a couple of times and never saw him again. The combination of the heat, the drugs, the pain, made me think that I was in a hospital room in Morocco—and to complete the impression, my doctor should have looked like Sidney Greenstreet.

Most of the nurses in the hospital were wonderful. Changing the dressing on my war wounds was as good a way as any to judge a nurse— for my wounds were tender and sore in the extreme; and part of the change was removing the old dressings from my testicles and putting on new dressings. That part of a man's anatomy is sensitive to touch anyway; so when there's pain there, it's really close to unbearable. There is, of course, no time for false modesty in a hospital. The surgeon who headed the team that reconstructed my privates was a black woman; most of the nurses were women. I was a bit of a medical curiosity. So I quickly lost my sense of embarrassment, and didn't care who changed my dressing so long as it hurt as little as possible. A number of nurses worked on me, and I saw them day after day. There was a Japanese-American; an American of Asian-Indian extraction; there were a number of blacks, a surprising number of whom were African and not African-American; but only a few Hispanics and men. There seemed to be far more Hispanic doctors than nurses, even though a great many of the patients at County are Hispanic. The team that came around to visit most of the Hispanics was bilingual, but only a few of the nurses spoke Spanish. For some of the patients, this was a real hardship.

My team of doctors was headed by Jacobs, a Jew; but it also included Amany Farid, a young woman doctor from Egypt; a Turk; and the previously mentioned plastic surgeon, Nathalie McDowell, a black doctor from the Virgin Islands.

I don't want to minimize County's problems, most of which relate to budget. Everyone damned the surgical gloves, which ripped and tore and often had to be thrown away. Most of the nurses and doctors were convinced that although they were cheap, they weren't cost effective, or medically effective. It was one of the many little disconcerting things at County. There is also racial tension, but mostly tension from being too overworked. At one point the pharmacy staff overloaded, and simply closed the pharmacy's windows. It was reopened by popular request by a phalanx of armed security guards.

Some of the black nurses were hard on Latinos who didn't speak the language—or who didn't at least attempt to speak the language. One black nurse was particularly tough on an El Salvadorean youngster, who, it is true, didn't understand her. This nurse was not the gentlest of nurses when she worked on my wounds, and she seemed sort of cold and unsympathetic in general. But I saw her early one morning with my most immediate neighbor, a black gang member who had been riddled with gunshot wounds in his stomach; he was a most unsocialized character, who never so much as nodded hello to me the whole time he was there. He had cowed most of the nurses, but not this one. I sensed that he offended her sense of hard-won middle class propriety: she too had probably come out of a tough inner-city ghetto and believed that was no reason to be unsocialized. So she summoned up all her authority, which was considerable, and let him know that she thought he was just a bad seed and that there were a few rules he had better start following. The first one was to call her "Nurse," and not "Hey you." She treated him like the bad kid he was. He ended up treating her with respect.

Early one morning toward the end of my time there, I struggled out of bed to walk down the hall. A high emphasis is placed on getting recovering patients out of bed, so that they don't catch pneumonia. But when you just feel like lying in bed and sleeping as much as possible, walking down the hall is a gargantuan task. I was seriously thinking of turning back after a few steps when the nurse suddenly called out to me that it looked like I was doing much better. There was genuine excitement in her voice, and it made me aware that I was actually recovering. She might have seemed a kind of dour person, but she had cheered me up. I might have felt wobbly, but I was in fact walking after having been horribly cut up in places that very much affect walking. I ended up taking a much longer walk than I had originally intended. Maybe the nurse wasn't my favorite, and maybe she was a bit too tough for my taste, but her instincts were those of a healer.

The original occupant of the bed on the other side of my bed was of the poor white persuasion—a department store salesman from Rosemead. I forgot exactly what he was in for; whatever it was, they had operated on him and he was recovering. To make conversation, I asked him what he thought of the hospital food, expecting the usual grunt and humorous aside about how bad it was. Hospital food, especially at County, is wholesome, I suppose, but not always appetizing. This fellow, however, began telling me how much he loved it—how he waited for each meal. It seems that on his wages, after he had paid his rent, he couldn't really afford to eat. He was always a little hungry. Sometimes, he proudly told me, he treated himself to a meal at a fast food emporium, which he considered haute cuisine. Then he told me about his life. He had been kicked out of the Army after 12 years, so the federal pension he had been expecting was gone. Now his greatest dream in life was one day to study at night school and become an accountant.

After my friend from Rosemead was gone, my next neighbor was Mr. Smithie, a black man in his early 60s. He was being treated for stomach ulcers, a hopeless task considering that his pancreas was done in by too much drinking, and in any event controlling the ulcer by diet was close to impossible since he preferred a liquid diet. Mr. Smithie was an obviously intelligent man with a well-worked out, fatalistic attitude about life and booze.

He had been around. He knew the difference between good and bad food. He said he had once been a caddie for Sam Snead or someone like that, that he had played cornet with trumpeter Freddie Hubbard as a youngster in an Indianapolis high school; I believed it. Mr. Smithie listened to a jazz station all night. He was a bright, cool dude, a real hipster philosopher and observer of the human scene. He was realistic about himself and his future; he had an almost joyful desire to get out of the hospital, go down to Main Street where all his friends were, and take his first nip. He also was planning when he got out to bum his way back to Indianapolis, to see his relatives.

Mr. Smithie—that's how he insisted on pronouncing and spelling it—was a good conversationalist and a very likeable man even if he was inevitably going to return to the street and continue his descent into a drunken maelstrom that would probably kill him in short order. He also felt a lot of disappointment about his life. He particularly liked the doctor who came around to see him because the young man was studious and probably was going to live a full, productive life. Mr. Smithie seemed to be sorry that he hadn't done the same thing. The young doctor appeared to be seduced by Mr. Smithie's considerable charms, and tried to convince him to go to a rehab farm rather than back to the street. Even when the young doctor was advised by other doctors that no place would be likely to take Mr. Smithie, because he had already been to all of them, he tried his best to see Mr. Smithie restore his life.

Mr. Smithie noted that he had often been involved with famous and rich men, but it hadn't made him rich or famous—even though, in all truthfulness, Mr. Smithie had every bit as much personality as Red Foxx, and many of his pithy observations were more cogent.

County is not perfect. I went to the outpatient clinic a number of weeks before anyone thought to monitor me for diabetes, the disease that brought me there in the first place. I had mentioned it to other doctors at the clinic, but no one had done anything until Nathalie McDowell was on duty. "You mean you haven't been monitored?"

"No, that's why I'm mentioning it."

She got on the phone and moved heaven and earth to get me into the diabetes clinic, and sent me downstairs for a blood test to see if there was anything to worry about immediately. I should have been monitored, although Dr. Jacobs patiently explained to me that my diabetes was probably adult onset, caused by being overweight. It would probably be possible to control it through diet. In any event, he added, while the body is healing, one can't get accurate readings for diabetes control. Still I wonder if the system would have gotten snagged on a glitch and forgotten to monitor me, without my speaking up.

Most of the people who work at County are conscientious, but it's a big system, and the patient has to take some responsibility for his care.

I guess in a way this country does have a kind of socialized medicine and I owe it my life. I will never again think of that building as a building of death. Rather, it was built in the spirit of the New Deal, with a sense of political enlightenment that has too long been missing from the body politic of this country. What's a society for, if not to guarantee everyone the right to good medical care, even if not everyone can afford it? What's a society for, if not to make a certain social contract with its citizens? There are certain minimal things: schooling, housing, health and transportation are the major reasons to create a civilization. You can't bottom line those things; if you do, the society suffers as much as the individual.

County Hospital was begun in the '20s, financed by local bonds. By the '30s the bonds were exhausted, but the hospital was finished as a WPA project. The building may be a little down on its uppers, but it remains as a reminder of that grand public manner of democracy which was the art and design spawned by the Great Depression.

It is not a building of death but rather of life.

© 1998 Steve London

*In this photo, photographer Steve London shoots the author*
*behind the wheel of a 1948 Cadillac.*
*The author's mentor, Scott Newhall, also was frequently*
*seen tooling around in classic cars.*

# Citizen Newhall:
# The Other California Editor

ou can put me down in the religion box as a California bohemian. And now let me offer a prayer for California bohemianism, by telling the story of the last great frontier journalist, Scott Newhall.

"A Great City's People Forced to Drink Swill," the headline read, and throughout Baghdad-by-the-Bay on that day in February 1963, in restaurants, cafes and corner delis, the townsfolk stared into their morning coffee and contemplated their bondage to an inferior bean. And then all hell broke loose as java met journalism for a California version of the Boston Tea Party.

The paper was the San Francisco *Chronicle*, and the man responsible for the story and headline was Scott Newhall, the editor who had transformed a comatose newspaper into the vital and fiercely independent journal that battled Randolph Hearst's old *Examiner* for the readers of a city and won.

Like other famous Newhall news stories, the "Swill Crisis" was born out of a sense of the absurd and bizarre. Newhall explained it this way to me in one of our many conversations about newspapermen and newspapers. "The Swill Crisis was about coffee—it told how horrible the coffee had become in San Francisco, of the filthy, rat-infested conditions that prevailed in its brewing in all too many coffee shops, especially along the main drag, Market Street." Newhall got the idea for the story when he went back east to be a Pulitzer juror. He drank coffee in a good hotel and realized how good coffee should taste and how long it had been since he had tasted anything like that in San Francisco—which especially bothered him, since the coffee trade was then the town's single biggest business.

When we talked about the "Swill Crisis," Scott hadn't been writing much about coffee, or even President Reagan (one for whom Newhall had a special loathing when Reagan was merely governor of California). In the early '80s Newhall was obsessed only with rebuilding his fire-gutted, grandiose, ornate, terribly eclectic Victorian mansion in Piru, some 45 miles northwest of Los Angeles. After throwing one of the grandest parties in the world (it really rivaled the shindigs thrown by the Great Gatsby), celebrating the completion of the new mansion as well as his 50th anniversary with his wife Ruth, he began slipping into a fatal gloominess as the age of Reagan-Bush began, undoing the tradition of the Roosevelt New Deal during which he had obviously developed his own sense of social justice and fairness.

Understand, this controversial newspaperman was the last representative of the colorful tradition of frontier journalists of the 19th century. His mentors were men such as Mark Twain, Ambrose Bierce, and Lucius Beebe. In the '80s Newhall still contributed occasional editorials to the Newhall *Signal* (of which he was then the editor, although no longer the owner, having sold out to the Morris newspaper chain), but the shock of Ronald Reagan becoming president stayed with him all the years the man was president.

I remember during the rebuilding of the mansion house, Nigey and I visited Scott and Ruth. They were living temporarily in a rambling English Tudor-style home in downtown Newhall, some 15 miles from the Piru Mansion. It was no accident that Scott Newhall and the town of Newhall shared a common last name, of course. Henry Mayo Newhall had given the town its name in the last century. W.C. Fields had once survived Newhall's arid summers in this same abode, with the aid of three built-in bars. His ghost was everywhere. As Newhall and I sat talking in the backyard, there was a rustling in the tall trees. I looked up and was greeted by the ominous sight of numerous huge ravens (at least the size of Thanksgiving turkeys) roosting on the tree limbs. Newhall grinned. No doubt he had entertained startled guests in this manner before. "It's their home," he said nonchalantly. "I hope they're not symbolic of anything."

Newhall was spread across a long cement bench—after a while you got used to the fact that Newhall sat and stood differently than most of the rest of us do. That was because he had a peg leg, the result of a mishap involving a horse in the jungles of Mexico many years ago. The leg developed gangrene, and, legend has it, Ruth had to cut it off, without anesthetic. (This was not strictly the case, his wife says.) Whatever, the wooden leg had added to his legend, for it gave him a characteristic stance—practically a trademark—a dramatic Ahab-like pose. Toward the end of his life, Newhall moved with a weariness that was evident in his voice as well. But his face remained young—and in the 25 years or so that I knew him, he hardly seemed to have aged.

He went from being the eternal optimist to being quite despondent about the nature of newspapers. As he talked while the ravens kept guard overhead, Newhall admitted to feeling something like a dinosaur.

Here he was, editor of the Newhall *Signal*, just another chain newspaper at that point, talking about his unhappiness with what he called "corporate newspapering." For newspapering had changed dramatically since 1952, when he assumed control of the San Francisco *Chronicle*, which then had the lowest circulation of the city's then four daily newspapers. He built it it into the state's second-largest circulation newspaper, which it remains to this day. While still editor of the *Chronicle* in 1962, Newhall purchased the *Signal*. He sold it in the '80s.

"I've been in the newspaper business since the Great Depression, and here we are teetering on the brink of another. If I weren't something of an optimist, I'd say the situation looks hopeless," he offered. Still, he insisted, somehow the nation—in his view with the help of its newspapers—had survived Nixon, and it would somehow survive Reagan and whatever else would come along. By the end of the '80s, he seemed to have given up hope on newspapers' ability or will to preserve freedom. They had become as much a part of the problem as the venal politicians who shaped the last years of his life.

Said Newhall of Reagan: "I've been watching him a lot on television, and he hasn't changed. He's the same fellow he was on the screen, where it was always the good guys against the bad Indians. He wants to be this century's General George Armstrong Custer—Reagan's last stand. Have you ever noticed that he gives a press conference and he's always in a polo suit or a hunting suit, or a cowboy suit. He makes his remarks, and then he's off riding into the sunset." On another occasion, Newhall wrote "The Ballad of Ron the Knight," which declared, "If you ever have the chance to get a look at the real man behind the pancake makeup and the carefully rehearsed clichés of the chief executive of the State of California, our State Constable, Ronald Reagan, you will find a quivering bowl of human jello who is desperately afraid of two exquisitely simple things— an educated man and an intelligent question."

In comparing Reagan and President Richard Nixon in 1973, Newhall wrote, "Where Richard Nixon is truly a mountebank, Ronald Reagan is simply an unctuous and unprincipled ass. Where Nixon talks of peace and covets the Nobel Prize and then bombs Cambodia, Reagan talks of trimming California state expenses and then lavishes millions on his personal jet plane and fraudulent expense accounts. When Nixon buys oceanside villas on the slightest whim and enriches himself beyond dream, Reagan has to content himself with living in a temporary mansion. Where Nixon's tax evasions are legal, Reagan's tax avoidance is only inspired."

On yet another occasion he described the state legislature as "a whining, lying, groveling gang of sneak thieves." The San Fernando Valley was "a heaven on earth for winos, dog poisoners, child abusers, husband swappers, wife-beaters, porno stars, bail jumpers, street racers, defrocked priests and street corner bordellos." Not only was his prose frontier-style, so were his actions. Three years after he purchased the *Signal*, he and his sons Skip and Tony personally faced down a Ku Klux Klan leader during a white-power rally in Saugus, after he had called out its leader in the pages of his newspaper. He got a vote from many of the local residents for being courageous, if nothing else.

Still, Newhall resisted being defined as the last of the frontier journalists. He was complimented by the description, but refused to believe it. "I'm just old Scott Newhall," he protested. "I have a personal belief that every one of us freezes at some age—some very old, some very young. I froze when my tennis was at my best, when I was 17. I'm vaguely irresponsible, always hopeful—it's been pretty hard to see a 17-year-old as an editor of stature."

It could not have just been coincidence that Newhall became editor of the newspaper to which Mark Twain himself, the godfather of the California bohemian movement (originally composed largely of newspapermen), had contributed in the 1860s. Newhall notes his bohemian kinship by describing a possibly prophetic event in his life that occurred while he was sitting in Hanno's, the bar across the alley rom the rear of the *Chronicle* building. "It was in the '30s, before the war—World War Two, not Three—and this wino came in off Skid Row, looked at me and suddenly began shouting, 'Jack, Jack! I thought you had died. Jack! You've come back!'" Newhall said that the wino was talking about Jack London, the most famous California bohemian next to Twain, adding, "I think I did look a bit like London."

Newhall believed that to find really superb newspaper writing, you had to go back to "old American newspapers." To Newhall, writing was the key point—and if anything is destroying newspapers, in his view, it isn't television so much as it is mediocre writing. "Newspapers will die if the writing comes out of an assembly line, if the newspaper isn't an arena for the written word. If you can maintain beautifully written words in newspapers, then newspapers will last forever."

Newhall doesn't blame the lack of good writing on the new generation's illiteracy, but on the way newspapers have been taken over by conglomerates. Profit-minded conglomerates, he says, have no real beliefs or principles. Corporate newspapers—which are becoming more and more ubiquitous these days—have "no heart, no soul." Their editors and publishers are interchangeable—they make the mistake of pandering to the advertisers.

To survive, Newhall believed, newspapers had to be provocative, colorful and intelligent—qualities that made for a winning *Chronicle*. Newhall says he saved the paper by giving it back to its creators: "We decided that we were going to get every writing talent we could, and we put together a remarkable group." He mentions such *Chronicle* regulars as Stan Delaplane, Herb Caen, Art Hoppe, Lucius Beebe, Warren Hinckle, Allan Temko and Charles McCabe, among others. Even in the '90s, some of these men are still writing. But most are dropping off, and certainly the *Chronicle* has lost its pizzazz.

Part of the successful formula Newhall created for the *Chronicle* was his ability to tap into the fairy tales we all grew up with. Thus the paper had treasure hunts and a "Fat Venus" contest in which a 250-pound girl was sweated down into a glorious svelte creature, the progress of which was faithfully chronicled in the paper over a two-year period.

He describes how the paper created Abigail Van Buren (of the syndicated "Dear Abby" fame) as its advice-to-the-lovelorn columnist in answer to her sister at the San Francisco *Examiner*. "One day this attractive girl with a mink down to her ankles—you never saw so much mink on one body—came in and said she wanted to write an advice column. I asked her what her credentials were, and she replied that she was Ann Landers' twin sister." Newhall hired her, and gave her the monicker Abigail Van Buren.

Newhall's peculiar fascination with monickering might have stemmed from the fact that his own name carries clout. The Newhalls, who originally hailed from Saugus, Massachusetts (which is why the town next to Newhall was called Saugus; both have now been lumped under the name Santa Clarita), were an old California land family who got their start in Gold Rush days, much as did another California land family whose name became connected with newspapers, the Hearsts.

It did not go unnoticed by people that Newhall always did things in an obsessive, Hearstian way. After quitting the *Chronicle* in 1971, Newhall spent most of his personal fortune aboard a century-old, steam-driven sidewheel tugboat named the Eppleton Hall, taking it across the Atlantic. Newhall purchased the boat, which had uneventfully lived out its life on the River Thames in London, and six months after setting sail (so to speak) from there, the expedition steamed under San Francisco's Golden Gate Bridge. The Eppleton Hall is now on permanent exhibit near San Francisco's National Maritime Museum, of which Newhall was a main founder and director. Another of Newhall's preoccupations was vintage Chryslers from the mid-'50s: he drove all over the state, reclaiming them, sometimes part by part, from junkyards from Sherman Oaks to Modesto, until eventually he had two warehouses full of them in Berkeley, as well as a fleet at the Piru mansion house and at the Newhall Signal. Then, in the early '70s, Newhall ran and lost a race against the incumbent San Francisco mayor, Joseph Alioto.

These were but a few of his crusades and obsessions. In the '80s he and Ruth, a partner in most of his ventures, concentrated on rebuilding the old Piru mansion, which was, not without good reason, dubbed "The Poor Man's Hearst Castle." It had been the scene of lavish parties that seemed to rival some of the tales of the grand days of Hearst Castle. Before it burned down, I attended some of the most memorable parties there that I had ever seen. Guests ate elaborate meals on a long marble-topped table, talked about politics, politicians and philosophy, and swam in the tiled pool outside.

All of that came to an end on February 18, 1981, as the result of an accidental fire started by a painter's blowtorch. The only thing left standing was part of the tower—a great three-story affair made of gray stone from a nearby quarry. Lost in the fire were more than 30 large stained-glass windows, many chandeliers and silver objects, and a couple of bed headboards made with inlaid panels of jade and opal, as well as 4,000 rare books, mostly Californiana.

The evening that we talked to Scott at W.C. Fields's old house— we talked about what it was that made a few great newspaper editors truly great. "I'm not going to sit here and try to defend Hearst," Newhall said, "because I did my best to destroy him for many years. I disagreed with everything the man said, wrote, did or the way he behaved." But then, in a moment when he was inclined to give the devil his due, Newhall made a rare confession: Hearst, he acknowledged, was a powerful editor and personality. Hearst, who was, of course, the prototype for Orson Welles' Citizen Kane, "did it his way, as they say nowadays, and when he died, his intellectual empire died with him. He conjured up his own newspapers, and when I got involved with the *Chronicle*, I too felt that we had to go our own way, and it was going to work or it wasn't. We were fortunate in that it seemed to work." Along the way, the *Chronicle* surpassed and trounced the San Francisco *Examiner*, which had been Hearst's flagship.

Newhall's *Chronicle* editorship was not without its detractors. Media critic Ben H. Bagdikian, a managing editor of the Washington *Post* and a professor of journalism at UC Berkeley, once denounced Newhall's reign at the *Chronicle* as "the weirdest circus in American journalism." Bagdikian referred to Newhall as "the evil genius of fun and games." Bagdikian's view was that Newhall had "no faith in the readers' intelligence and did not take journalism seriously. Unfortunately, he had talent." Bagdikian particularly complained about the Swill Crisis. To him, it showed that Newhall had only a frivolous sense of news.

Having worked as a reporter on the *Signal* and later the *Chronicle* under Newhall, I can testify that Bagdikian was wrong. Newhall believed that honest writers were like members of a priesthood, holding aloft the mirror that reflects truth, even if people hate the truth. Newhall considered newspapers literature—"daily literature" is how he defined real newspapering. If there's anything that would save us "from the final follies of humanity," he thought, it would be newspapers.

He also thought, however, that newspapers that take themselves with "deadly seriousness" are wrong. A newspaper, he once observed, "should be as pleasant and companionable and informative and entertaining as anyone in your family, or anybody you pay to go see on the screen." Newhall revealed his art school background when he said: "One has to assume that we are all pretty absurd, although that word means different things to different people. When one takes himself totally seriously, he's in trouble. I'm sure Ronald Reagan takes himself seriously, and that's why we are in such trouble. One has to have a sense of humor."

Newhall also pointed out that while Bagdikian criticized the *Chronicle* for not being a serious newspaper, in point of fact the *Chronicle* under Newhall's editorship was the only major newspaper in the country to consistently oppose and fight McCarthyism in the '50s and the war in Vietnam in the '60s, right from the beginning—not later when it became fashionable to do so. "*The New York Times* finally discovered that we may have made a mistake in Vietnam. We said it was a mistake from the day anyone was sent there. Ours was the only paper of any size that fought loyalty oaths, so that people like Ben Bagdikian could teach in a free environment. We fought alone on that."

Having lived a while in Southern California (although he maintained a condominium in San Francisco), Newhall said that it used to be that "there was a lot of substance in San Francisco, and it was all done with mirrors in Los Angeles. Now there's a lot of substance down here, and the mirrors seemed to have moved north."

If anyone should know what was substance, and what's done with mirrors, Scott Newhall should.

In 1992 Nigey and I went to the mansion house for his memorial service. It was not meant to be a sad occasion. It was a kind of Irish wake, in a way (although Newhall was as English as they came, despite the fact that he could have been a double for Jack London). And at first it felt almost like a party—there was a jazz band (Scott had been a passable stride pianist, and in the '60s he had singlehandedly resuscitated the career of Earl "Fatha" Hines, the greatest living stride pianist). After 25 years, it was nice to make contact again with people I had known who had been a part of Newhall's world. Folks from all walks of life, who had been touched by him, got up and gave their testimonies of him. And despite the fact that they were talking in the past tense about Newhall, I half expected Newhall himself to walk out of the front room, as if the whole thing had been a joke. There was a big part of me that wanted to join the others in talking about Newhall, but I couldn't. Suddenly the old mansion house seemed forlorn—its ringmaster and curator was gone, and perhaps it knew that it would not survive for long without the devoted (if maniacal) care of its creator.

I suddenly felt as if none of us would survive long without Newhall. Even Ruth, tough, resourceful—the only person who could have been his match and mate—seemed overwhelmed, even though she was the master of the stiff upper lip.

The passing of Newhall from this earth was not something that should have been. There are some people who should live forever. I felt as if I were leaving a big part of me behind when I left the mansion house, never to talk with the last of the frontier journalists, again.

# Syd Cassyd's TV Wars

ince the earliest days of my Inner Sanctum, I've been in the habit of reading Marxist and atheist tomes and feeling wicked about doing so. I'm definitely one of the seemingly dwindling number who thinks that Karl Marx was right about most things. I can't think of anyone who has ever better explained the dynamics of history than Marx. He was a great visionary. Class struggle is the motif that explains most of human history. But there are, of course, other factors. Race and gender are issues, for example.

Still, Marx was right in talking about the Industrial Revolution. He's dated some when it comes to cybernetics and other modern technologies, whose basic impact has been to make the theory of the surplus value of labor seem redundant.

Do not misunderstand me. Do not be too quick to jettison the Industrial Revolution. Cybernetics will change it, but not eliminate it. Things will still need to be manufactured. And services will still need to be performed—all the more if totally automated manufacturing really becomes the norm.

If human labor is the source of all wealth—which is a most reasonable concept—what happens when computers enable one to extend his or her human labor power a millionfold by using the machine. Human labor will be extended; there'll be more of it; and it will not be scarce.

A new vision has to accompany advancing technology. Best it be a democratic and humane vision. One vision that accompanied the beginning of television originated with Syd Cassyd, who had a very prophetic view of the new medium.

One of Cassyd's main points is that the public airwaves should not be controlled by a market created by greedy broadcasting monopolies for only their own purposes. What a lot of people don't understand is that those who have appropriated ownership of the public airwaves have to be complete idiots not to make money with them.

Cassyd is one of the few prophetic people I have known. The other one was Jacque Fresco, whom we will talk about in the last chapter of this book.

The honorary chairman of the 50th anniversary celebration of the National Academy of Television Arts and Sciences is also the man who founded the academy on a back lot of Paramount Studios in 1946.

There was a time when no one would even admit that he had founded the academy. Cassyd was always a gadfly, a critic of the industry, but a true lover of the medium.

And some of his old concerns returned when the Academy did not invite him to the 50th anniversary Emmy show in Pasadena in 1996. It wasn't that the Academy didn't recognize him. Officials had turned up for the planting of his star on Hollywood Boulevard a few weeks before the 50th Emmy show. Then they turned up to praise him. But perhaps they were concerned that if he was at the actual event, he would say some things on international television that would embarass them. Perhaps in their own minds they used as the excuse that Cassyd does not get around very well because his Parkinson's disease is now well advanced. Whatever the reason, he was not invited there—and he was upset about it.

The honorary chairman always was an infuriating scatterbrain. You ask him about one thing, and part-way through his answer he's off on something else. Off he goes mid-sentence, rummaging through his shelves of papers in his den, finally pulling out a yellowed clipping about some cause or other he was in the middle of, or a letter from somebody at the White House, or City Hall, or Drew Pearson, or a commendation from a mayor, governor or university.

For many years, Syd Cassyd's den was even more full with material on the history of television. But then one day in the '70s they carted off three van loads to the Syd Cassyd Archives at UCLA. Cassyd's archives sat on the shelves at UCLA until 1990, literally gathering cobwebs, and worse, not being catalogued. When the curator was asked about this, she complained that Cassyd "had the money, he should have paid UCLA to maintain them."

With that, the archives were moved to the Academy of Television Arts and Sciences, located in North Hollywood, where Cassyd was given a hero's welcome, and the papers are maintained with the devotion and care that one would have expected California's once great university system to have lavished on them.

That possibly softened Cassyd's opposition to the Emmy (television's equivalent of the movie industry Oscar), the statuette that the ATAS is most famous for. He's won at least a couple of them himself, most recently the 1991 ATAS Syd Cassyd Founder's Award. He now finds himself invited into the inner sanctum of the academy, which still contains representatives of the big corporations that run the industry—but also includes such a famed gadfly as himself, and the president of one of Hollywood's biggest unions, AFTRA. In the old days, labor would not have been allowed in even by the side entrance. Cassyd also finds significance in the fact that the academy's current executive director was Jim Loper, who founded public television station KCET. Cassyd's big concern always was that television's highest and best use is as a tool of education. He points out that today's high school student spends 15,000 hours at school, and 17,000 hours watching television—and that alone is reason enough for lots of concern.

He's excited because "all the dreams of the '30s and '40s are now coming true—satellite television, interactive television, new technologies that allow, for example, instant access to the libraries of the world."

In a way, he believes he's won his biggest fight—against the deregulation of the Reagan era, which in Cassyd's view was just an attempt by the broadcast networks to keep their dominant place, despite changing technologies. For practical effect, the networks were trying to void the Federal Communication Commission's original mandate to operate broadcast facilities on the public airwaves for "the public good" instead of just for the bottom line. Although the FCC was dominated by a venal and corrupt broadcasting industry during the Reagan years, their position of dominance is now being undone by changing technologies, such as cable, phone lines, satellite dishes, and now the Internet, Cassyd believes.

Cassyd also notes a couple of other changes, including increasing foreign ownership of Hollywood. "NBC is now owned by General Electric, which is owned by Thompson of France. There are big changes with the international cartels," he says, "and with Hughes getting into satellites, there will be more changes." He observes that the big broadcasting moguls who controlled the nation's airwaves got everything they wanted during the Reagan years, but are losing their dominance anyway due to technological changes.

At the heart of Cassyd's message was always an explicit question: Who gave these people the control of the people's airwaves? When the federal government grants a corporation the right to run a television station, it does not exact a tax or fee. Cassyd points out that the airwaves belong not to the networks or other broadcasting stations but to the people as a whole. It might not appear that way, because along the way the airwaves were usurped by the broadcasting giants who obtained the rights to use them, and in effect to own them. The airwaves are a natural resource just like the nation's rivers and forests, Cassyd insists. Cassyd points out that, by law, television and radio were supposed to be operated "in the public interest, convenience and necessity." Were this the case, Cassyd adds, there would be no need for public television stations like KCET in Los Angeles.

There's something about the way Cassyd goes about doing things that tells you he has been a gadfly of no inconsiderable effect in Hollywood for many years—a man who has been a mover and a shaker in his way, but never rich or powerful. The longer you know Cassyd, the more you begin to see that it's not that he's scatterbrained, he's just moving on too many fronts. After a while, you see all the different projects really are of a piece.

Cassyd was five years old when he played a newsboy in an early silent picture made in New Jersey—in 1914. He's been involved with what they now call Hollywood even before he moved to Los Angeles. Along the way, he's been a stage producer (he did a version of "Tobacco Road" with John Carradine); he also produced such early award-winning television shows as "Young Musical America" and "Candy's Playhouse." And he produced the third Emmy show in 1950, because he not only founded the Academy of Television Arts and Sciences, he was its fourth president then.

Primarily, he's made his living as a newspaperman. For many years he was the West Coast office of *Box Office* magazine, the trade journal of the theater owners since 1919. Until recently, he is still busy writing a column in a local newspaper and Hollywood columns for publication in such diverse places as Mexico City and Japan.

Cassyd became more housebound as a result of various maladies not totally unexpected in a man in his late '80s. Cassyd vowed, "There's nothing that can keep me from working, from doing a lot of thinking." He couldn't do as much lecturing at various universities as he has in the past, but he carried on as a consultant, and a lot of people still call him. Some he charged for his advice, and some he didn't.

Most days, even in his 80s, Cassyd was up at 5 a.m. reading the newspaper, working at his typewriter, or making phone calls back East. You could find him similarly occupied in his den as late as midnight. Even now, in his 90s and in poor health, suffering from Parkinson's, among other maladies, Cassyd keeps at it.

He says that the best answer to what he has been doing all his life came one sunny day in Jerusalem in 1976. He was standing before the Wailing Wall, when he suddenly became very aware of his Jewish roots as he looked at the wall and walked through the archeological excavations under it. Despite the fact that he is not religious, what he saw was the timetable which gave his life meaning.

Cassyd said: "I remember looking up at the young Israeli soldiers standing guard on the walls of Jerusalem and thinking of their counterparts, centuries before, who had blown their horns, warning of the coming assaults. Archeologists digging at the temple sites have been unearthing more and more of the story of the two temples, the second of which was built on the foundations of the first.

"I saw suddenly with extreme clarity that here was an analogy between the history of the two temples and my own life. I'm making no claims to being a Solomon, but in 1946, I was the catalyst and founding member of the National Academy of Television Arts and Sciences—and then as I stood that day before the Wailing Wall, I realized that the Academy had been modern-day America's first temple of television."

For many years, Cassyd angrily thundered at the Academy he founded, particularly at its Emmys. But over the years, the Emmys have gotten bigger and bigger, the award ceremony being sent to hundreds of millions of television sets in the United States and now nearly half a billion throughout the world. For a long time, Cassyd regarded the Academy as little better than a chamber of commerce for the television industry. "Our Nebuchadnezzars were those in commercial broadcasting who seized the entire Academy and its apparatus, destroying our first temple's goals and ideals. Their false gods were gold statuettes, which held aloft a globe symbolizing the birth of the atomic age," he once said to me.

It has been noted that Cassyd himself is the recipient of two Emmys. When I first went to his house in the mid-'70s, one was headless. He was using another Emmy for a doorstop; it was a hot summer afternoon. Though he has often said the high financial stakes of the Emmy had warped the Academy's purpose, even then he was actually rather proud of his Emmys. How could he not be? One was given to him for forming the Academy in the first place. Cassyd held the broken Emmy and said that one day he would get around to getting it fixed—the same way, I sensed then, he'd like to get the Academy itself fixed—and these days when he talks about the Academy, he does so in the tone of voice of a father, talking about a somewhat errant offspring he still loves, because it is, after all, his own.

Cassyd formed the Academy in 1946, only a few months after he arrived in Hollywood. He came into town, still in his Army uniform, with his wife Miriam and sick child, in the upper berth of a Pullman compartment, and $100 mustering-out pay. Within two days, he had a laboring job on the back lot of Paramount on Melrose Ave.

One of the sound stages at Paramount had been turned into a pioneer television station, which later was to become KTLA. Cassyd was immediately attracted. He devoted his nights to organizing the Academy. His original vision, he says, was for the Academy to be just what its name implied, a place for people to present ideas which could be thrashed out in a democratic forum by those with other viewpoints. By the time the Academy was going, there were only 4,000 television sets in the Southland, and those were mostly in bars. A 10-inch receiver in those days went for $350, which was a lot more money then than it is now.

Like many other television pioneers, Cassyd saw television as an incredible tool for good, for enlightenment, for education, for democracy and against war. He now admits that was maybe too idealistic a hope.

Cassyd realized that to make the Academy work he needed a name more famous than his own to head it. So he chased after Edgar Bergen, the ventriloquist, who was then big in radio but was fascinated by television. Bergen became the Academy's first president. He then tried to get Cassyd to become his administrative aide, but since there were only enough funds for a half-time salary, Cassyd had to decline. Miriam, however, went to work as the Academy's first secretary. Every year they picked a new president, and in 1950, Cassyd became the Academy's fourth president.

The issue of democracy was important, because that was one of the reasons that the generation returning had just fought a war for democracy against the Nazi beast. More than once Cassyd proposed that the Academy should spend $35,000 and have a regular national membership meeting by closed circuit television. If the Academy members cannot confront and deal with the real issues, Cassyd says, then the Academy is little more than tool of "those who fill our airwaves with junk entertainment for quick profits."

The Academy is now controlled "by the powerful groups producing the junk on television," he charged. Cassyd originally had envisioned part of the Academy representing the consumers of television. It quickly became apparent to him this was not to be the case. In 1967, he tried to create a National Academy of Television Receivers. The proposal generated a lot of enthusiasm, but Cassyd was without the means to make it a dream come true. Nonetheless, he believes his organization helped inspire the consumer movement in general.

Cassyd is a deeply political man. He was born into a family involved in both politics and the theater arts. His father, Leon Cassyd, whom he visited on the East Coast as often as he could, became a lawyer in 1903. Leon was from a distinguished family that included ambassadors as well as theater moguls.

Not only did Cassyd work around films and television, he also has been a department store executive, an aide on Wall Street, and an investigator on New York Mayor Fiorello La Guardia's staff fighting Tammany Hall. There were less glamorous times. He was broke during the Depression too. But what Cassyd is the proudest of is the fact that he has a "50-year perspective on television."

Syd discovered the labor movement and the related labor theater movement during the Depression. He was involved in the Loyalist cause against fascism in Spain. He was also an instructor and consultant on educational films at New York University, and has worked around universities in other capacities despite the fact he doesn't have a high school diploma. He produced early educational television shows in New York before the war, and during the war worked as a film editor under Colonel Frank Capra.

With this background, it is not surprising that Dr. Linus Pauling, the two-time Nobel Prize winner, hired Cassyd as an aide. It was 1960—Pauling was trying to get individual governments to stop plans to test atomic weapons in outer space. The United States Senate was deeply split about Pauling's efforts, and the Defense Department was furious at him. Pauling had decided he could take the heat for speaking out because his reputation as a chemist—some say the greatest ever—was secure, whereas other scientists were more vulnerable to pressure.

Pauling organized not only the American scientific community but those of other countries as well, including the Soviet Union. Eventually, the world scientific community presented the case to the UN and the result was an international treaty banning outer space testing. To Cassyd, Pauling was next to God, a brave and courageous man as well as a great scientist.

One of Cassyd's best memories of his six months working with Pauling was when the scientist gave him several thousand dollars and sent him to Carmel to scout out a place for the Linus Pauling Institute. The money came from Pauling's first Nobel Prize. Cassyd searched out various estates in the Carmel area, but the Linus Pauling Institute had to await its birth until some time later. Pauling became occupied with fighting off political attacks on him from the nation's capital for his advocacy of a ban on nuclear testing in outer space.

Another side of Cassyd is that of archivist—he is dedicated to the preserving of historic records with all the intensity he devotes to his politics. One of his projects involves tracking down and making copies of kinescopes, 35-millimeter films shot directly off the screen. Many of these old TV shows have been lost, he says, because the local Musicians Union wanted all copies of TV programs destroyed 30 days after they were shown. The union feared that producers would cannibalize the music from old soundtracks rather than pay union members to make new music. Unfortunately, because of the 30-day rule, a lot of early television was lost, Cassyd says. He has helped promote projects to save what kinescopes there may still be.

As Cassyd talks, you can feel what those early days of the Academy must have been like. Cameramen argued with the heads of the networks. It was a kind of democracy that the moguls were not so thrilled with, but it existed in those early days anyway.

The worst thing about the Emmy was that it finally attracted the covetous eye of Ed Sullivan, the king of variety show hosts during the so-called Golden Days of television. As a Broadway newspaper columnist and variety show host, Sullivan made no bones about the fact he felt he had been slighted by not being given an Emmy by the Hollywood-based Academy. His show, "Toast of the Town," had won an Emmy, but Sullivan himself went awardless.

To Cassyd, Sullivan represented not the best of Gotham, which after all had been Cassyd's own home before World War II, but the big corporate interests. When Sullivan successfully staged what Cassyd describes as a "coup" and took control of the Academy away from Hollywood, it was the Emmys he coveted. By-products of the move were the loss of democracy for the membership and some heavy-handed rewriting of history. When talking of the latter, Cassyd compares Sullivan to Stalin.

On St. Patrick's Day, 1957, shortly after the Sullivan coup, Cassyd was in New York. It was just after the parade, and Cassyd phoned Sullivan from a booth on Fifth Avenue. He had been given the number by one of Sullivan's employees who thought things might be patched up between Hollywood and New York. Sullivan answered Cassyd's courtesy call, however, with 15 minutes of the most abusive invective Cassyd has ever taken. It was so loud that at times Cassyd had to hold the phone away from his ear. He listened in amazement as Sullivan told him he would never work in television again. Sullivan also bellowed he was going to fire the man who had given Cassyd his phone number.

Cassyd said he found out many years later Sullivan did indeed fire that employee. Sullivan also told Cassyd that if he made any statements about the Academy to the New York newspapers, he, Sullivan, would denounce them. Cassyd left the phone booth shaken and amazed, but figured maybe Sullivan's ranting was due to too much St. Patrick's Day cheer.

The next day, however, various New York newspapers blossomed forth with stories saying, among other things, what a horrible fellow Cassyd was. Cassyd still has those clippings. In one story, Sullivan complained that the Academy and its Emmys had been founded by a fan magazine publisher—he meant Cassyd. Cassyd said he was indeed the editor of a television magazine, but it certainly was no fan magazine. Nonetheless, the story became gospel after being repeated by such august publications as the *New York Times* and *TV Guide*.

The "fan magazine" story was particularly ironic, because Sullivan had sponsored a counter organization to the Academy. Sullivan's academy, however, was a profit-making company owned by friends of his who did indeed publish a fan magazine. This fan magazine began issuing Michaels, which were meant to be the equivalent of the Emmys. But despite the fact Sullivan won Michaels, they never gained the reputation that the Emmy did.

So Sullivan went west to a meeting of the board of directors of the Academy in Hollywood. And in the end, Sullivan won. The Academy was given a new constitution which created a "national association" that was no longer controlled directly by the members but by appointees from the chapters.

Sullivan was after the Emmys. The original ideals of the Academy were meaningless to him. Therefore, says Cassyd, Sullivan had to simply eliminate the first decade of the Academy's existence. From 1956 on, the Academy's official literature had listed Sullivan as the first president.

Cassyd takes out two identical looking white pamphlets. Both have an embossed Emmy and beneath it the same logo. But one was produced before 1956, and the other came out after 1956. The old one says the Academy was founded in "November, 1946, although the idea of it was born in the summer of that same year in the mind of television editor Syd

Cassyd, who was then newly out of the Signal Corps. He was later to be the Academy's fourth president in 1950." The new one says: "November, 1946, in Hollywood, and became a national organization in 1957."

Quipped Edgar Bergen, the first president, after looking at the pamphlets, "It's like saying Washington was not our first president, for we had only 13 colonies."

Cassyd wrote his full version of the Sullivan coup in his history, "Emmy Awards Confidential," which was produced on a $2,000 grant from the Hollywood Chapter of the Academy in 1977. At that time, the dissension between East and West seemed to have flared anew, and the Hollywood chapter was looking for documentation that it, as the founding chapter, owned the Emmy, and not the 1956 association that Ed Sullivan formed. Cassyd was the only person with all the documentation of this, so the Hollywood chapter asked him to write an account. Cassyd did so, along with some editorial help from this reporter and Nigey Lennon.

"Emmy Awards Confidential" was virtually impossible to find for a while. Cassyd and his two editorialists delivered 100 copies to the Academy office and not another word was heard until the '90s, when NATAS took over the Syd Cassyd archives from UCLA, which had so badly botched the job. The great dispute of 1977 was worked out not by the various members of the Academy but by both sides' respective lawyers. Today the Academy has been reconstituted for a third time, and in its present incarnation is located in North Hollywood where the Syd Cassyd archives are.

Cassyd will sometimes say good things about some of the Academy's current activities that are not so far from what he originally envisioned. He thinks the Academy's *Emmy* magazine is top-rate, for instance. Nonetheless, he was upset at the fact that *Emmy* would not run an article from him on the lost decade of Academy history.

Cassyd points out that television is now on the brink of such far-reaching changes that the next 50 years are going to make the first 50 years look like nothing. For years, Cassyd had been writing about direct satellite-to-home disc antennas, videodiscs, cable and the like. Two-way television has an incredible future, he believes, as does telephone television. One could research the world's libraries at the flick of a finger for information, or print out a book with two-way television. The new technology will make the networks redundant. He thinks the monopoly of NBC, CBS and ABC over the airwaves is due to come crumbling down—deregulation was merely the way they hoped to fight that.

With deregulation, station owners no longer would have to meet any standards of minimal quality, Cassyd pointed out. Television stations would be automated to the point no one would be running them but an advertising sales force and an engineer. Also, deregulation would have given the present owners of the airwaves such monopoly controls, they would effectively be able to hold back the exciting new technologies. Still, they cannot succeed, Cassyd told me. "Network television is about to lose as big a share of the entertainment dollar as movie studios did when television cranked up—which was a lot."

In 1959 Cassyd was named curator of television at the Los Angeles County's ill-fated Hollywood Museum, across from the Hollywood Bowl. "The Hollywood Museum deserves a book of its own," he says. "Actually, Universal Studios ended up as the instrument through which some of the dreams of the museum were realized. Universal capitalized on the ideas envisioned for the museum and built a theme park around the notion of showing people how films are made."

Cassyd is proud that he is one high school dropout who did well, who worked with a great Nobel Prize winner, who's been a lecturer and consultant at almost every Southland university, and was even a dean of extended services at a college. His phone still rings with people seeking advice and information. Until very recently, he has continued writing about Hollywood.

When I first wrote about Cassyd in the *Herald-Examiner*'s Sunday magazine in the '70s, I mentioned the decapitated Emmy. So the Academy gave him a new Emmy, to replace the old one. And when he gave away his Syd Cassyd Archives, he by no means gave away everything. He still keeps a lot of his stuff in his study at home. His life remains a work in progress.

# Unpopular Science

*I* hope that your trip through my Inner Sanctum has been an instructional one. I know that in this day and age, being either fat or a Man of the Left is not popular. The term "Party Line" now makes more sense when used to describe the ideological direction American mass media hews to than any Soviet party line. The mantra of the market has become the only one allowed.

Anyone who mentions that, maybe in the mix, some concern for institutions and individuals who live by values other than the bottom line might also be appropriate, is looked at with suspicion. Poets, musicians and pure scientists are all suspect, unless they find a way to sing the proper anthem.

As long as the First Amendment is still alive, I want to continue singing the song of real prophets, and hopefully that's what I'm doing in this book.

There is Experience and Innocence, just as there are different sorts of cities with different souls. New York and Los Angeles are competitors and counterparts, and from each of their cesspools a different kind of effluent flows.

Personally, I was more attracted to Chicago, but for me it remains the most inscrutable.

My sense is that Chicago is more honest, more real, more physical, in its soul. It was built on beef and steel and concrete and wood. New York produces the dominant culture, and for that it should be eternally damned. Los Angeles is, well, just is. It will always be the capital of the West, and some rivalry will always exist with New York as each produces its culture. The fact that the Los Angeles basin is defined by the very substantial San Gabriel Mountains means there's always a mountain range in the background. And it's an archetypal range, suggesting the thinness of the veneer that civilization really is. It sits there laughing at the puniness of human endeavor all the time. Whatever it is that is laughing —some would call it God—it is the fearful symmetry of its grin that is forever etched in each of our Inner Sanctums. After all, what are these mountains but creations of the San Andreas Fault that runs through them.

In the case of my parrots, Nick the Professor, Hamlet (better known as Hammy), Wuzzie, Bubba, Girlie, and Cutie, I long ago realized that I like them as much as I do because I'm part of their flock. I am a creature just sitting around in the post-Jurassic. The birds stand on two legs; so do I. They understand when you're feeling bad, or they're feeling bad, and they have strong emotional individual characters. The odd thing is that a flock does not seem to emphasize the sameness of its denizens, but their differences.

And by the way, since our visit is about over, close the oaken door on your way out please.

Where the Golden State Freeway now streaks past the Los Feliz district near Griffith Park, once stood the laboratory of a brilliant, self-taught scientist named Jacque Fresco. Fresco had a circle of disciples who considered him next only to Albert Einstein, although the friends and relatives of those disciples often thought Fresco was a fraud and charlatan.

The laboratory was a prefabricated affair made of aluminum. Earl "Madman" Muntz, who as well known around the City of the Angels, was an admirer of Fresco's. He had asked Fresco to make plans for building prefab industrial facilities and to construct an actual prototype, in which Fresco got to live and work free as payment for his work. In the early '50s people in Los Angeles didn't exactly cotton to nonconformists like Fresco, who was a dark little man of exotic foreign extraction who had the temerity to wear a beard. Invariably someone would bait Fresco by asking him why he wore a beard. And invariably he would reply, "Why do you shave?" Fresco believed that the burden of explanation should be placed on his questioners—the ones who shaved the natural hair off their faces.

Perhaps in conformity with the tenor of those times, Fresco was not so bold as to admit to the world at large that he lived in an aluminum house. So the laboratory was sprayed with a stucco paint and, at first glance, looked almost conventional. The inside of the lab was warm and rather dark, except where illumination was needed. The icebox was always filled with good things to eat. You entered the laboratory through its kitchen and then walked into the rest of the dwelling. Drafting tables were found in the living quarters as well as couches, which doubled as beds. Fresco's disciples often sat on those couches during marathon sessions with their guru. Behind the living quarters was the actual laboratory. It had a workshop, of course, but there was also a dark gallery full of strange things like oscilloscopes and an optically-produced three-dimensional image of a giant fly such as you'd see under a microscope. Unlike the 3-D movies showing in those days, you didn't have to wear glasses to get the effect. In a way the fly was a kind of early hologram, although Fresco's invention used a different principle than the laser beams used in modern holography.

The motif of all of Fresco's work, however, was the flying wing. The flying wing was Fresco's truth, Fresco's stamp. He built plastic models of the flying wing. He drew endless drawings of flying wings and when he was in the Air Force, the Air Force patented some of his flying wing designs. In Fresco's many pictures of futuristic cities, there were often flying wings circling overhead. Fresco had been drawing flying wings since the early '30s, and when John Northrop was actually building flying wings for the Air Force in the late '40s, he and Fresco would argue about their design. The Air Force patented but never used the radical wing structure that Fresco had invented, and Fresco felt Northrop should have used it in his flying wing. Northrop was the only early airplane builder Fresco respected; perhaps the two men had a special rapport because neither graduated from school. Fresco was not unknown in the early days of the aircraft industry. As a Douglas aircraft employee, he had argued with his chief engineer about an airplane design. Fresco warned that it would crash during its first big test. It did, killing two people.

The story of the flying wing is better known these days. Along the way, Clete Roberts did a show on the subject for Los Angeles public television station KCET, and in it he revealed for the first time how Stuart Symington, Truman's Secretary of the Army Air Corps, had ordered the destruction of Northrop's seven prototype flying wings—despite promising test-flight results. Roberts also quoted from a new National Aeronautics and Space Administration report that predicted the flying wing was about to be rediscovered. All of which reminded me of what Fresco used to say all the time—that airplanes were built wrong. He argued that if you needed to build a wing huge enough to support a fuselage for people and freight, why not just make the wing itself larger and stronger and put the payload inside the wing? He said that airplanes built in wing shape would be far more stable and efficient.

Fresco truly did not see the world like most men. He saw everything in a very radical way, so radical that he boasted he made Communists look reactionary. In the early '50s I went to Fresco's laboratory every Saturday morning, supposedly to take lessons in technical illustration. But Fresco was more than just my drafting teacher—he was my mentor. Imagine how a man who told you that airplanes were built all wrong would make you look at everything else.

At one point during the Depression Fresco had been attracted to the theories of Karl Marx. But he finally decided—and was brave enough to declare as much at a public meeting of the Young Communist League, from which he was physically ejected—that Marx was all wrong. Fresco felt that Marx was no longer accurate in talking about human labor being the source of all wealth, for one day, Fresco said, machines would make human labor redundant. It was a matter of simple physics. A man working all day long is lucky to produce a third-of-a-horsepower's worth of work. Machines will one day do everything a man can do, only better, Fresco said. Besides, he asked, what else was man but a rather inefficient machine at best?

Aviation and cybernetics were but a couple of Fresco's many interests. At the heart of all his concerns was a deep and abiding anti-mysticism. He was a disciple of the pioneer biologist Jacques Loeb, the original "mechanist."

Fresco made you look at the world through new eyes. The things Fresco told me seemed to make so much more sense than what my teachers said, so I was always arguing with them. In all the years since I had last seen Fresco, I have realized over and over again what a profound impact the man had on me. And I began to wonder. After all, I was hardly a boy of ten when I knew him. If he was as much a genius as I had once thought, why had I heard so little about Fresco all these years?

The Fresco saga started re-entering my life after I hadn't seen him in nearly 30 years. Around the time of the Clete Roberts program, I was contacted by a Dr. Jack Catran, a scientist who wanted me to write about his new book, *Is There Intelligent Life on Earth?* To publicize the book, Catran had been on radio and television attacking astronomer Carl Sagan's theory that there is life on other planets we should be trying to contact. He even had a retort to Sagan published on the op-ed page of the *New York Times* under the headline "NASA Scientists in Orbit."

Jack Catran, then in his early 60s, has been many things in his career. He once did a short stint in Yiddish theater. Then he was able to bill himself as a space scientist, which wasn't an unfair designation if you considered the different technical and scientific skills he's employed in years of working around Los Angeles's aerospace industry. He concluded his career in aerospace by doing the human engineering on the Apollo project, the rocket that first landed men on the moon.

Catran propounded a couple of at first seemingly unrelated theories. The first was that there is no intelligent life in outer space—that was just plain wrong. Catran's second theory is that the source of all economic, social, and political ills on this earth is the money system, which is inevitably going to give way to a technocratic utopia.

As I leafed through Catran's book, something about his theories seemed awfully familiar. I read the book's acknowledgment page and quickly found out why. Among the list of Dr. Catran's mentors, including such luminaries as B.F. Skinner, Charles Darwin, Albert Einstein, Alfred Korzybski, and Ivan Pavlov, was the name of Jacque Fresco. Was this, I wondered with a powerful sense of amazement, the same Jacque Fresco I had known as a child? Could there have been another Jacque Fresco?

A call to Dr. Catran quickly confirmed we were indeed talking about the same Jacque Fresco. Fresco, Catran told me, had moved to Miami in the mid-'50s, after the State of California had destroyed the laboratory to make way for the Golden State Freeway. He became something of a local celebrity in Florida, and by 1969, a New York publisher had brought out a Fresco-inspired book entitled *Looking Forward*. The book didn't do well, and Fresco was not terribly happy with how his co-author had written up his idea of what the future would be like.

When we met a few days later at his home in Sepulveda, Catran told me he had been worried. Fresco's phone in Florida had been disconnected. He hoped Fresco was all right. It might just be that Fresco was broke. He always was broke. It was apparent that Catran feared something worse than being broke had occurred to Fresco.

Fresco was not just Catran's mentor—he was also his boyhood chum in the Bensonhurst section of Brooklyn, where the two grew up together at the bottom of the Depression. Fresco was the first to leave the old neighborhood and come to Los Angeles, in 1939. Catran followed in January, 1941, and was only one member of a "gang" of neighborhood chums who followed Fresco west. Most of the old gang went on to successful careers as lawyers and such. And most of them ended up rejecting

Fresco as a great genius. Only Catran believed he had remained true to
Fresco's dream of science. The love of science was a strict and passionate
thing with Fresco, a love that was further distinguished by a correspond-
ing hatred of mysticism, in which he included animistic projections of all
kinds, from God to Santa Claus.

Guess who else came out of the Bensonhurst section of Brooklyn,
only a few years later? Catran grinned. Carl Sagan. Catran admitted that
he might feel especially strongly about Sagan because those were the same
streets where he was first imbued with the vision of science as the great
truth that vanquished all mysticism. Catran believed a gigantic error is
behind Sagan's obsession with extraterrestrial life. You might call it a mix-
ing of science with the camp of the Opposition—the mystics, the religion-
ists. Not only is Sagan in error, Catran said, but worse, he thought Sagan
was also committing "b.s.—what I call bad science." Sagan, Catran
added, has a basic problem understanding such terms as "life" and "intelligence" in a scientific manner.

"I expect to be sued by Sagan in the near future," Catran
declared, even though he said he's unsure whether Sagan was even aware
of his existence. One national television show did try to arrange a debate
between the two, and it wasn't Catran who turned them down. "He's an
astronomer," admitted Catran, "a smart boy, well educated, quite bright, I
really have nothing against him personally. But he's dealing out a lot of
nonsense in the area of extraterrestrial life to the many readers of his popular books. Either he's doing it for book sales or, worse than that, he
believes his own stuff—at least partially."

Catran began writing his book as a rebuttal to an article by Sagan
in *Scientific American* that suggested the possibility of intelligent life in
outer space. Catran gave his article the title, "Is There Intelligent Life on
Earth?" and over the years the rebuttal to Sagan grew into a book. "You
don't expect intelligent life in outer space for the same reason you don't
come across a New York dialect in the jungles of Africa," he said. But
even if there is life on other planets, "it could just be a pulsating blob of
protoplasm, belching radiation."

When Sagan assumes "intelligent life" would want to communicate with us—or even think in those terms—Sagan is suffering from nothing more complex than a case of "elementary anthropomorphic projection," Catran said. The best example of this occurred when Sagan succeeded in placing time capsules aboard Voyager I, and the earlier Pioneer
10. They were designed to tell intelligent space aliens in other solar systems what Homo sapiens is like. Catran sneered when talking about the

contents of Voyager's package, which included a phonograph (with instructions) and records that featured a message from President Carter and music from Bach to Chuck Berry. He was even more derisive of the six-by-nine-inch aluminum plate etched with a drawing of a man and a woman by Mrs. Sagan that was placed aboard Pioneer 10 in 1972. The couple had their arms raised in greeting to aliens. Catran pointed out that if one were to greet someone in this manner in the Middle East, the greeting would be taken as an insult.

About the matter of communication with space aliens, Catran dismissed it with a laugh. Scientists who speak Chinese and English can't speak precisely to each other even with translators, Catran said. But Catran emphasized he did not object to the space program itself, not only because he worked on the Apollo project. But he said that instead of spending billions of dollars on futile attempts to find intelligent life in outer space, he would rather see the money spent on solving man's problems here on earth, which is the second premise of his book. He argues that the money system is now in collapse and must be replaced with a technological system, based on resources. A big premise, of course, and we talked about it in great detail as soon as I determined that he was talking Fresco's old talk. But first he wanted to finish up the Sagan matter.

He said that Sagan and the National Aeronautics and Space Administration are thinking sentimentally, if not mystically, about life. "There is no soul for a surgeon to see when he cuts the body open. What the surgeon sees is what is there—blood and tissues. The very ideas of will and desire, of intent and motivation, are unscientific. We are controlled by natural forces just as much as a tree is. Our insides are just as much a part of the universe as the rings of Saturn. What appears to be intelligence is really just a behavioral response to forces outside of us. The intelligence differences between individuals is minor. What we all are is the sum total of our genetic endowment and our conditioning, our environment."

Catran is, obviously, a behaviorist. And indeed, his academic degrees, including his doctorate, are in psychology. (Fresco was also a behaviorist—when I knew him, his language was full of words like "conditioning" and "tropism" and so on.) Catran believed the only scientific work being done in psychology is by the followers of Harvard's B.F. Skinner. Catran suggested that Sagan would be well advised to study his Skinner.

Sagan's assumption that one day aliens and Homo sapiens will have a universal meeting of "nice, thoughtful, pipe-smoking scientists is ridiculous," Catran said. "They are merely looking at themselves." In

Catran's view, Sagan and company are not acting so very different from how "the anthropologists say our ancestors acted when they first invented God. Man started to believe in God thousands of years ago when he was walking around and suddenly thunder and rain began to pour. Early man did not know about natural phenomena so he thought a guy up there was mad at him and that's why it was thundering and raining and lightning. So he got down on his knees and said, in effect, 'Lay off, I'll be a nice guy.' He would have been a whole lot better off if, instead of praying, he had tried to learn about natural forces."

Catran is proud his book is the first by a scientist that argues that "talk of extraterrestrial life is insufficient science." Indeed, he adds, it is the first book by anyone that argues against the concept of intelligent life in outer space. Catran says that Sagan is not aware of the recent discoveries in behavioral sciences that define knowledge and intelligence. "It used to be thought that a rock fell because it had a desire to reach the ground," Catran says. "That was animism, where one ascribes life to objects. The psychologists are the worst—they talk about spirits and desires in even more extravagant terms than the old Greeks did. The fact of the matter is the leaves of a tree turn toward the sun because of photosynthesis. Caterpillars are geotropic—where they go is determined by gravity."

Similarly, says Catran, animals and people are tropistic. "We move by responding to natural laws," Catran says, although he later amends this slightly by saying that Jacques Loeb, the biologist who first propounded a mechanistic universe, did not prove to be right in all his particulars.

To Catran, Sagan's desire to communicate with intelligent life in outer space has as much meaning as attempts to talk to the sun or the trees right here on earth. "Why doesn't he want to try to talk to the sun? The sun is much older than we are—surely it must know the secrets of the universe. Or how about communication between us and trees? Even Sagan talks about chauvinism, by which he means the danger that we might use earth terms to describe life forms on other planets. He calls it oxygen chauvinism when people think that extraterrestrial life has to breathe oxygen. I agree with him when he talks about these different biological chauvinisms—but he hasn't carried the idea far enough. For we also have life and intelligence chauvinisms to deal with."

To assume that extraterrestrial beings would have ears and mouths and ways of "communicating" is not to understand how evolution works, Catran says. "What Darwin was all about was about how change occurs by mutation and then survives. If the environment can support a particular mutation, it survives. If not, it dies. You could draw pictures of every conceivable kind of life that ever existed, and it probably did exist on this planet at one time. The configuration of our species developed over millions of years of mutations—in other words, by chance, by accident. If you eliminate man and started all over again, he would not come out like we are now.

"It appears as if everything we have was designed for a purpose. But the truth is, if we had three arms, we'd find a purpose for three arms." Catran also warns that man shouldn't give himself too much credit for intelligence because he thinks. "What we know as thinking is merely covert speech," Catran said. He also disputed the prevailing notion that our brains are computers, with memories in a central file. "What is called memory is merely changed behavior. Behavior is not an expression of thinking. It is the thought. I know this runs contrary to everything people know, but we really are pushed and prodded through life. I know on a certain level it looks as if man has will, that a man is really courageous and brave, but this is really not the case."

So what is the truth according to Catran? Men are machines and not very efficient ones at that. Men make machines that work better than man. A 747, explained Catran, who early on worked for Douglas and Hughes as an aircraft engineer, doesn't imitate a bird and flap its wings. "It does a hell of a lot more. It flies through the air for thousands of miles carrying people and freight." The whole basis of cybernetics—the science of men and machines invented by Massachusetts Institute of Technology mathematician Norbert Weiner shortly after World War II—is that anything a man can do, machines can do better, Catran said. Both Fresco and Catran were enthralled with Weiner's cybernetics theory, for it fit in well with their theories of mechanism, which had arisen on the streets of Brooklyn a decade or two before.

Catran allowed himself to wax sentimental when he talked about the old Brooklyn neighborhood where intense discussions of things like science and technology, politics and culture, filled the air. "The Depression was a tremendous time to be alive in Brooklyn. There was so much intellectual ferment. The library was always full of people studying, trying to get out of the ghetto."

The Depression in a strange way was a liberating influence from not only the ghetto but also from religion. To Catran and Fresco, science was the new religion. Although Fresco was born in Harlem in 1917, both Fresco and Catran lived as a minority in a minority. They were Arabic Jews, members of a little pocket of Sephardic Jews among the East European Jews. Fresco's parents had come from Istanbul and Haifa. Catran's parents came from Damascus and Tangier. They spoke Ladino, not Yiddish. Ladino is Spanish with a little Hebrew thrown in. The Arab Jews were regarded as strange and uncouth by the East European Jews, Catran remembered. The religion of the Sephardic Jews was even more orthodox and superstitious than that of the most unenlightened East European ghetto Jew. Furthermore, the Sephardic Jews were even poorer than their East European counterparts. Catran said his father looked like "any old Arab."

Catran was 15 when he met Fresco, who was 16. From the beginning, Catran looked up to Fresco, if for no other reason than that Fresco was a year older. They met when Fresco heard that Catran collected landing gear, propellers, and similar parts from World War I airplanes. Catran had just obtained an eight-foot propeller Fresco wanted. It had come C.O.D. $2, much to father Catran's annoyance. To get the propeller Fresco offered Catran all the balsa wood he could use, drawings of models of World War I airplane models that Fresco had personally designed, and one other thing. The "other thing" clinched the deal, Catran recounted. Fresco offered Catran a prized possession of his brother's—a metal, sheepskin-lined jock strap. "I couldn't resist the offer," Catran said.

Then Catran received his first lesson in science from Fresco—a lesson in physics. After agreeing to help Fresco carry the propeller home through the streets of Brooklyn, Fresco placed Catran at the middle; Fresco picked up the tip. Catran ended up carrying most of the weight. Catran hung around Fresco more and more. Not only did they talk science all the time, but Fresco also convinced Catran to drop out of school. Fresco never got past elementary school. "It was all bullshit to him," Catran said. "He had been put in the back of the class, where he spent all his time drawing cities of the future."

Catran believed Fresco's lack of formal education may have been "a happy accident for him." It meant he had no great respect for textbook authority, Catran argued. "Education can be a kind of trap—I described formal education as a trap in my book," he said. I nodded, remembering how Fresco's flying wing had first affected me. There I was, an impressionable lad, even younger than Catran had been when he first met Fresco.

And he was telling me that many things done by authorities were done wrong, that airplanes were designed wrong, that they should just look like great wings. Fresco had me questioning authority so often in school I was becoming known as a "discipline problem." I guess I've remained a discipline problem ever since.

It was Fresco who gave me my first good, powerful dose of atheism, which I've modified only a bit on the inexorable road to senility. As Catran and I talked of Fresco, it was apparent how powerful an exponent of atheism he had been. Catran said his parents hated Fresco not only because he convinced Catran that school was a waste of time, but also because he had made an atheist out of their son. One fine day many years ago, it seems, Fresco had asked his brother Dave Fresco (who became a character actor in Hollywood), what an atheist was. Dave told Jacque that an atheist was someone who denied the existence of God. Fresco went on to research atheism, and not only declared himself to be one, but tried to turn everyone else into one too.

Catran eventually went back to school after the war in Los Angeles, but his atheism was never lost. "Look at the Pope," Catran said in high dudgeon. "Look at the starving people on the streets that he's dragged through. If he were a decent guy he'd be ashamed to go out there. They carry him on a throne—you'd think he'd take half of all that money and give it to those starving people." Adding real insult after injury is how those with religious and mystical views use the gifts of technology like television, microphones, and computers to sell the opposite of science. And although Sagan is a scientist, Catran believes he has sold out and made himself part and parcel of the mystical cabala.

The greatest indignity of all is that Catran's own daughter liked to attend witchcraft sessions in Hollywood, replete with candles and Tarot cards. "My own daughter," he repeated a couple of times, sounding incredulous. To Catran, astrology, the occult, religion, gurus—it's all superstition.

"I know why people are moving away from reality and rejecting science," Catran said. "Reality is a pretty horrible thing in the United States today. Our cities are slums. The air is polluted. And people still believe in angels and devils in this world. Look at the millions out there in Latin America, still dominated by the Church. And then there are the Buddhists, the Muslims, the born-again Christians. The majority of people in this world really are lost. They're still seeing that thunder and lightning in the wrong way. The more aware we become of natural phenomena, the happier our lives can be."

❖

For a long period in the '30s, the "gang" gathered at night on the roof of Fresco's building in Bensonhurst. The conversation was science. Of the original group, Catran said he is the only one who had remained true to Fresco's philosophy. In the '80s the gang still met from time to time for "nostalgic" reasons, and the last time they did they all wondered how Catran could have acknowledged Fresco in his book alongside Einstein. Catran unhesitantly replied: As great as Einstein was, Fresco is his equal.

Catran believed Fresco left for Los Angeles just a little too early—that he should have waited to see the World's Fair in New York in 1939. "It was the world of tomorrow where the future is very beautiful," Catran said. Fresco had always hated Brooklyn—it was too cold. Once as a lad he hopped a freight train to Miami and returned home to Brooklyn raving of the sun and palm trees. Similarly, all through 1939, Fresco sent "the gang" letters from California extolling its warmth and palm trees. After a while Fresco also discovered technocracy and added that to the reasons Los Angeles was better than Brooklyn. And Catran understands why Fresco left here in the '50s. Not only had a freeway run down his home, but it was also getting smoggy. Fresco wouldn't live in the smog. He wanted to live in the tropics.

Catran remembered his first impression of Los Angeles as he alighted at the old Greyhound Bus Terminal downtown. It was January 1941. "I got out of the bus after a trip of four days and five nights, or what-ever it was, and it looked like New York, which I thought I had left behind." Catran was greeted by a couple of Bensonhurst gang members who assured him Los Angeles was not at all like New York or Brooklyn. They told him to wait until they got to their house in Hermosa Beach to see what they were talking about. But first they warned Catran that, to make room for him, they had to kick out a young woman named Harriet. Before giving up living with five or six males, Harriet shook her fist at Catran. But finally she was liter-ally thrown on the street, with her large diaphragm (in those days diaphragms were much bigger than they are now) right behind her.

Catran moved in and now all of the old gang around Fresco was ensconced in Hermosa Beach. But not for long. Since a number of people were living on one salary (one of the gang had a production job in an aircraft factory), funds were short. When the rent was due, the gang had to do a moonlit flit—goodbye, beach living.

The gang then proceeded to live in a number of houses around the Hollywood area. "Two guys would rent the place, and that night twelve would move in," Catran said.

"We made a lot of noise. You could hear Fresco working all night long—he was working with Lucite, which was then a very new material. It sounded like we had a factory going. We did, actually." Catran also remembered one day when things got so bad the finance company came to repossess the car. But the car's battery was dead, and the repossessor had to push it down the street. As they did, Catran remembers Fresco looking at the odd scene, repeating over and over, "It's only money, it's only money."

The gang was finally undone by women (poetic justice when you look at it from Harriet's standpoint). Catran said that women almost invariably hated Fresco; they felt threatened by Fresco's monopolization of their men. Ultimately they forced their men to choose between them or Fresco—there was no in-between.

Like everyone else, the gang had to face the war. One day Catran was driving to work at Lockheed in Burbank, when he spotted Fresco, looking the saddest he had ever seen him look. Fresco was standing in an Army induction line outside the Warner studios. Fresco's talents, however, did not go unnoticed by the Army. He was assigned to a special futuristic unit of the Army's Air Force where he drew all day. Fresco didn't adjust to Army life and was eventually discharged, but not before the Air Force had patented one of his designs—a different way of building the interior structure of an airplane wing, the same structure Fresco thought Northrop should have used in the flying wing.

The way a wing is built hasn't changed since the earliest days of aviation. Cloth or metal is stretched over parallel ribs that go from the wing's leading edge to the rear. Fresco's design had a central forging, from which the metal ribs emanated like spokes of a bicycle wheel. In theory the load is then distributed back to the central forging, making the whole structure almost unbreakable. Fresco told Northrop he should put the central forging of the flying wing's structure near the cockpit, but Northrop—who had himself been thinking of flying wings since at least 1929—rejected this advice. Or so Catran told it.

Catran said the closest Fresco ever came to being a public success was in the late '40s when Earl "Madman" Muntz spent $500,000, which was a lot more money than it would be now, on something called the Trend Home. Trend Homes, says Catran, were the gang's last hurrah. The idea was simply that a home of aluminum could be manufactured quickly and cheaply for all the GIs coming home from the war. Muntz regarded his investment as seed money—to have succeeded, Trend Homes would have needed federal money. A man from the Truman administration did come to look the project over, but still nothing came of it.

Fresco was not without his influential admirers. Forrest Ackerman, the well known science-fiction impresario, "who had a good scientific background himself," was always terribly taken with Fresco. "Not too long ago," Catran said, "Ackerman told me the country should just go ahead and make Fresco President to see if he really has the answers."

Not surprisingly, Fresco did make some money designing and building miniature scenes for "Project Moon Base," an early movie on space stations and moon journeys. He was the technical adviser on a number of other science-fiction movies. He made models in his Los Feliz laboratory, and as a youngster I remember how much fun it was to play with the ones that had been used in the movies.

Catran took the basic skills Fresco had taught him—drafting and technical illustration—and developed his abilities from them. He gained practical experience as an aviation engineer at Douglas and other aircraft factories, but he also took advantage of the GI Bill and attended Chouinard Art Institute. So he came to make a good living as an industrial engineer by combining his two talents. Then Catran went back to school and ended up, after putting in time at USC and UCLA, with a master's degree in psychology. In the late '50s and early '60s Catran got involved in a new field that came out of the aerospace industry—human-factors engineering. Indeed, Catran became the editor of the journal in the field, Feedback. He ultimately obtained a doctorate in psychology from the University of London, and was tops in his field.

It was a very logical career path for a former Fresco disciple. Catran admitted he'd done a lot of unlikely things. He couldn't resist telling his Howard Hughes story, for instance. "In the early '50s, I was one of the few guys who saw Hughes every day. I was styling his 'cunt wagon.' He had taken a Douglas I-20 and rebuilt the cabin so he could fly girls and booze between Arrowhead and L.A. I put a rug on the floor. Designed jazzy seats and put in bigger windows, which was a job. Bigger windows meant that the structure of the airplane had to be changed. I saw Hughes a lot but I can't say I had a lot of conversations with him. I'd joke with the other guys that Hughes had actually talked to me today. He had grunted at me to get out of his way. He was strange. He wore his sneakers and often didn't bother to zip up his fly."

Later Catran helped design rockets for the Apollo spacecraft. His responsibility was to approve all engineering so that maintenance crews as well as astronauts could work most efficiently with the machinery. As a result of his work as a human-factors engineer, Catran said, "I found my interests expanding to the design of the whole system—fitting people into the environment. That's the big system that one day scientists and engineers will have to turn their attentions to."

Admitting that his ideas might sound Cassandra-like, Catran predicted that "within a few years he was sure the whole money system will collapse. The transportation system will grind to a halt. Riots will break out—and the military might even be moved in." (Catran predicted all this considerably before the Los Angeles riots of 1992.) He went on to extrapolate that the inevitable outcome is that the military won't be able to cope any better than the politicians, and the result is that the scientists and technologists who are already manning the system anyway will be called upon to design new cities, in new locations. Most American cities are past the point of rebuilding, he said. They grew up too haphazardly, topsy-turvy, working on no design, no intelligence, mostly chance. The silver lining, the light that Catran sees at the end of the tunnel, is already here; it is the technology that surrounds us.

Today our technology is ill-used. Microcomputers, for example, weren't created for playing games on a TV tube. "We already live in a technological world, but we have an archaic way of using the gifts of this technology—the money system." Catran argued that financiers, accountants, lawyers, and what-not, will not exist in the future because these are professions that essentially perform no real function. "The United States is wealthy. We are surrounded by material objects. We could automate overnight and have an abundance of everything. What's getting in the way is the money system. It's strange how there's a fuss every time there's an advance in technology and people are thrown out of work. That's good— we should be liberated from work. But in the money system we now have, more technology only means more unemployment."

Catran dismissed the idea that there's virtue in the work ethic with the Fresco snort of "bullshit." He repeats: "We should be liberated from work. If anyone still really believes in the existence of the work ethic, they ought to stand outside the exit of a factory at 5—they'll get killed in the rush. Anyone would take more than two weeks vacation, right? What's wrong with three months?" Catran said it is nonsense to say people would get bored without dull, demeaning work. Not if they could get educated and travel and learn and enjoy instead.

Catran contended that economists are useless. "Nobody even knows what money is. None of these guys—from Keynes to Friedman— none has a clear explanation of what money is. Money is only needed when there is a scarcity of products. Technology could eliminate scarcity overnight. We have the factories to make the stuff but the problem is distribution."

Catran said that while placing the production of the country in the hands of engineers and scientists and other technologists might not appear democratic, the pilot of a plane isn't voted into office on the basis of a popularity contest among the passengers. Besides, Catran argued, "there's no worse dictatorship than the money system that limits what you can get. There's nothing more democratic than an equitable distribution system. For one thing, you'd eliminate 95 percent of all crime, because crime is the only way people who don't have anything in the system have of trying to get a piece of the action."

Catran said that economist Milton Friedman's arguments that giant corporations are merely responding to the market is just nonsense. "Look at television. They (TV programmers) create what they like. Art isn't reflecting society; in this case society winds up reflecting art. In fact with all the promotion of sex and violence, television is destroying many people's traditional values. Your likes and dislikes are created by Madison Avenue. I know—I was an industrial designer. First we would create the design and at first people might balk, but eventually we'd find a way to get to them. The truth of the matter is that it is very easy to sell anything in the United States today—for God's sake, look at the Pet Rock."

The fact that anything can be sold explains why mysticism is on the increase, he said. "The world of today is very painful. Our cities are slums and tenements full of poverty and pollution and crime. Mysticism is a beautiful retreat. Really, it's very tough being young today. I can see why dope has such great attraction. Today everything is out of control. It is collapsing. Mysticism sells."

Bleak as this picture may be, Catran does not believe the country is reverting to a Dark Age. "We know too much about electricity, aircraft, medicine, and surgery." Catran doesn't think you need look to history for answers, either. "What's so marvelous about the pyramids? They're a pile of rocks. Any corner gas station is a far more sophisticated structure than the pyramids." Suddenly Catran interjected the name of his old nemesis from Bensonhurst, Carl Sagan. "On one of those 'Cosmos' shows, Sagan talked about the marvels of Alexandria, Egypt, the library there. He unrolled some parchments. What the hell knowledge was in those parchments? Their astronomy was astrology. They knew nothing."

Catran said the society of the future would be a "very warm and human place, with far more freedom than we have today. There will be no dictatorship of things. People can have what they want. And there will be poets and painters and composers, entertainers, actors, and mimes. They will continue their work on an even grander scale, but it will be different. Our culture came out of the poverty era of man and that will not last, unless we're wiped out in a nuclear war first. The future's art will be far different from ours."

And Catran laughed. He began talking about how as a youth he saw Fresco only a couple of nights a week. On other nights he went to Greenwich Village and spent time around the bohemian scene. In the early '60s Catran was a habitué of various old Los Angeles coffeehouses such as the Xanadu and the Fifth Estate. He loved to argue philosophy and play chess with the crowd there. Catran thinks that the coffeehouse period in Los Angeles in the '60s was a real bright spot.

And he laughed again. "Frankly, I'll tell you something. I might not even be happy in the world of the future I'm describing. It might not be for me, but don't tell anyone that. That's off the record."

I finally got to talk to Fresco just a couple of years ago. One of the first things I asked him about was the flying wing. I remember that when the Stealth bomber was being rolled out of its hangar in the Mojave, one television report noted that the plane was not particularly stable—it required a lot of computerized controls to keep it aloft. Fresco snorted at its mention. "A terrible design. A lousy piece of crap. I have the answers in my designs." He does not blame the design on Northrop. The plane was designed by people who succeeded him, he said. But Fresco didn't really want to talk about the Flying Wing. "Lionel, people aren't interested in stuff like that. They are interested in the future direction of society." And Fresco would talk about nothing else.

Fresco now lives in Venus, Florida, where he is assembling his 22-acre model city of the future. He and his partner, Roxanne Meadows, are actually building the structures that he thinks will form the basis of the new cities that must be built if there is to be much of a future for mankind. His basic idea is that this city they are building can be used as the set for a movie about the future that will encourage the new cities.

People today are in many ways reflections, are clones of a society that lived 1,000 years ago, Fresco said. "We are preprogrammed to the dominant values of this culture." The basic problem, in Fresco's view, is that most people are cloned—by their parents, by their families, by their schools, by their employers, by their nations. "It has always been this way, he admits. If you're raised by headhunters of the Amazon, they will do away with you if you don't fit in." The same with the Nazis, he says, and it happens elsewhere as well.

Fresco is planning to write a piece one of these days called "Laugh, Clone, Laugh!" about his thesis.

"Of course children don't identify with the society," he emphasizes. "There's nothing but slaughter in the movies and on television. When they talk about the future, it's about space stations being blown up or creatures being killed by their intestines being ripped out. They can see chainsaw murders while they eat popcorn on Saturdays, but they can't watch adults having sex. You wonder why children have no feelings."

Fresco remembers when he was in elementary school he had a teacher who wanted him to "'think American.' I informed her that the beds we sleep in were designed in England, the language that we speak is butchered English, our religion is imported, and if it hadn't been for guys like Louis Pasteur, we wouldn't be here. The Arabs gave us the electric battery, the Phoenicians and Egyptians gave us much of good early science. All the way down the line we owe so much to so many from so many different lands." The teacher wanted him to pledge allegiance to the flag of the United States." 'Can I pledge allegiance to the earth and everybody on it?' She said, 'No you can't.'"

Ultimately Fresco was sent to the principal, who turned out to be a wise man. He gave Fresco his own place to read whatever he wanted, and he even took him to Macy's to buy him tools and materials to work with. He also said, " 'There is no place for kids like you in our schools.' He was a rare character," said Fresco. "Most institutions believe that the society can't be managed unless everyone thinks alike, and yet they are worried that a scientifically run society would be a dictatorship. But when you go to work for any industry, you are in a dictatorship. When you punch a time clock you don't do what you want to do. You don't vote on the direction of the industry. You manufacture fenders or headlights and when you leave, you exit to the right because there's a sign that says no left turn. We do not live in a democracy. We do have to look at the earth as a single system. When the Russians dump nuclear wastes into the water, it has adverse effects on all of us. There's no isolation anymore, and this world must be managed not by a technical dictatorship but by systems that keep the water and air clean."

Like Catran, Fresco expects that the money system is due for a major collapse, because although all the factories can be automated, few will be employed, few will buy the products. A moral lecture is not the answer; you have to modify the conditions that generate undesirable behavior. You can't work on drug addicts and then turn them back into the system where people have no feelings, no identification anymore, he says. Like Catran, he proposes that first the money system will collapse, and the army and police will be called in. "We have to surpass the money system and go to a resource-based economy. If we took all the money and gold in the world and dumped them off the coast of Japan, as long as you didn't take the top soil and other resources, as long as the factories and the minerals are still there, we will live. But even that won't be enough." Leveling the old cities and building new ones such as he's has been designing all his life is the only way to go. "People will see that in the film. The film will have people from this period brought into the future, so that you will see both today's values and the viewpoint of the future." From that he thinks people will join him in building an experimental city, and then the idea will just keep spreading—just as the automobile replaced the horse and buggy, not because people were talked into it but because there was no other way to go.

Fresco predicts that the military and police won't be able to control society when the money system collapses, because "people have known television sets, they've had things. Before the last Depression people had nothing. They lived in misery. They couldn't afford any medical care. So now people have known a little bit of the taste of glory. In this society, you help an old lady across the street and you feel good. Where the hell is she going when she gets across the street? The whole society has no direction, it doesn't even anticipate a direction." Fresco also denounces the whole idea of "honoring your mother and father. If we really did that we'd still be in caves. We should honor any human being worthy of honor, but if your parents are bigots or racists, that shouldn't be hidden." Children, he said, should not be raised by incompetent parents, but rather by those who truly love children, and have the expertise to raise them.

Fresco says that a lot of what he believes came from his Depression years, riding freight trains. "I'm talking Grapes of Wrath, I lived through that period. And if you don't become social out of that . . . that's a condition that shaped my values, being hungry on the road. That's how I build my identity. Those were social conditions that generated liberals; they don't exist in our society anymore. We're getting a bunch of meatheads because our society doesn't have the ingredients to generate sensitive people. Now we are living in the tail of the Middle Ages, the Land of the Living Dead."

I concurred. And then I brought up the subject of my birds—I know that Catran, as a mechanist, had a supercilious attitude to animals. I, on the other hand, am in danger of becoming one of those terrible people who loves my birds better than I love most people. Fresco actually is not a cold, technocratic man. He does a good imitation of really being concerned and sensitive. Maybe it's more than an imitation. I didn't feel like asking my childhood mentor to tell me why my love of my birds was just so much projection. So I tried for a deeper chord. Hammy was acting up in the background, and I apologized, telling him that I lived with birds in my bedroom and was quite fond of them. Which, of course, is a euphemism. I told him that this chapter about him was in a book I was working on.

"You know, birds are dinosaurs," I said, wondering as I told him this if that would be a wedge for a disillusionment from my mentor. "And I find that I'm very fond of them. They have accepted us as part of the flock, and that works well. Then when you think about birds being dinosaurs, well, that just gives rise to a lot of interesting things to think about," I said.

Before I could think this whole thought out, Fresco had quickly blurted out, "Yes, of course."

I did not go on. It was time to end the phone call. I doubt it will happen in his lifetime, but I hope people discover Fresco's work, even after his death, and get the ball rolling. But I confess I love this Ciudad de Los Angeles, San Francisco, London, Haifa and Jerusalem, and Sacramento as they are today. I already have terrible trouble with how these cities have changed in my lifetime. I'm not sure I can personally take any more change. I certainly wouldn't want to level these to start anew. Like most people, I don't adapt to change well. I find it terribly sad, most of the time. Old things I love fade away, to be replaced by new ones I don't like so well, such as blaring bassy boomboxes with their metal rock death sounds instead of Mozart. But I suspect that Fresco is right, and one day his city will be built—he has left enough notes and thoughts on it— and it will pave the way into a better future.

I realize that's my hopeful, even optimistic side speaking. The songs of experience are not as pleasant to sing.

Let me tell you, I've been working graveyard at City News Service, and that means monitoring the city's news at night and writing it up, mostly for the radio. I can tell you that typically five or six people are murdered on a weekend night. Most of the victims are in the black or Latino parts of town, of course, but not always.

You sit there with the dreary run of murders, most of them with victims who get a paragraph or so in a news story, and usually they are described as not having yet been identified, perhaps because next of kin have to be notified. Sometimes it takes a bit for the coroner or someone to makes the identification, and by then no one wants their names anymore. They're yesterday's news. Someone is gunned down for no reason other than that they were in the wrong place at the wrong time. We're still living in the Old West, here in Los Angeles. The nightly gunshots heard in many neighborhoods are testimony to that.

You sit up there and process all those words telling about the murder and mayhem in the city, and then you get really jazzed up when there's an earthquake because when the ground beneath you can shake like that, murders are too commonplace to contemplate.

But the commonplace happens every day, and can't be ignored. After the Northridge quake, Nigey and I took refuge in a 100-year-old remodeled carriage house. It seemed like an idyll of Los Angeles living— with lush vegetation, streaming sun, and even the wind and the rain.

Until one night, when I was awakened from a dream turned sour by a screaming voice, a voice so close it seemed to be right in my bedroom. Then I heard footsteps. Someone was running fast down the alleyway which hadn't been passable by cars in many years.

There was no way that person could do anything but run straight ahead, downhill, for all the structures adjacent to the alley had walls and fences.

He didn't run fast enough. The shooter ran just as furiously down the alley right behind him. And then, shots rang out.

The gunman carried a flashlight as well as a weapon. It took me a while before I realized where the tiny jabs of light, stabbing at the bedroom walls, were coming from, and it gave me the chills.

It was getting close to midnight, when I'd be due at work. Just then I heard a second round of shots, and the running and the voices stopped. Not too much later, a helicopter was whirring overhead, pointing its powerful beams on our house.

After a while they went away; cop cars came to the end of the alley. I didn't know what was going on, but there were lights and voices coming from there.

Then it seemed to get quiet again. I pulled myself out of bed and contemplated going out into the cold Hollywood night. I felt somewhat safer because there were still cops down the alley, taking care of business.

Later that night, Nigey told me after I left, and the cops left, she heard someone downstairs walking around. After several long minutes, whoever it was walked away. She realized the killer had been hiding under our house all that time.

That night I had asked a reporter at Parker Center to call Rampart Division and find out what had happened—it was not only news, it was of personal interest to me.

But the reporter couldn't get anything; the watch commander had just changed shifts. It wasn't until a few days later that she got some of the details, and by then, it was just too old to be news anymore. Just another gang shooting in Los Angeles.

Suddenly our little carriage house didn't seem quite the urban oasis it had been. It didn't help that on the first night, Rampart Division didn't even know what I was talking about.

I began to wonder if I lived on the alley in Los Angeles where people just disappeared. Unknown gunmen chased them down the alleyway and shot them before they reached the end. And nobody ever knew that it happened, much less who they were.

After that, Nigey and I joined the crowds of urban folks wondering how much longer we could stand to live in the city. The city had become like a prison for all of us. We traveled around contemplating other places. We checked out the tree-lined Victorian-era streets of Sacramento, and took a train trip to Chicago.

Looking at the other America, the non-urban America, we saw places in New Mexico and Kansas from our window. I thought about a relative in Australia, who lives on a sheep ranch, and was always inviting us to come out and live there.

After a while, however, enough time had passed so that the need to get out seemed less pressing. And then, finally, we moved to a new apartment up the street, and now everything seems fine.

And so I continue going to work, sitting there on the 19th floor of an office block in Hollywood guiding the news out into the night from the microwaves atop Mt. Wilson. I am the trumpeter of bad tidings—and sometimes a few funny ones—about the new day.

I'm like a rooster, noisily welcoming the sun every single day. Prophecy is everywhere first illuminated at that moment when the sun first casts its searching rays on all the terrestrial things that have been hiding under the cloak of night. But it's a very brief moment, soon lost in the advance of crushing daylight.

Eventually, though, we make a few of our dreams, some of the prophecy, happen.

*The late Walden Muns*

# Afterword

he year 1997 was not a good one for the author. First Rosie the dog died. Then Burbette, who was known as Girlie at the end, and who was our most wonderful person-pet-companion, died. Rosie and Girlie died from seizures in front of us. It was hard to watch, but I think it somehow was a better way for them to die than to die alone without their people.

Next, Monty Muns, who had been our housemate, was killed in a car accident. And then Nigey left me.

It was not a good year for dreams or hopes or even fighting the good fight. It was just a year to survive.

Muns, who had been a mainstay of the Los Angeles' coffeehouse scene of the '60s and a poet, journalist and raconteur, had been the manager of the Xanadu Coffeehouse near Los Angeles City College. Muns and the coffeehouse were a transitional institution between the beatnik and hippie in the early '60s.

As I've mentioned, the nation's first underground newspaper, the Los Angeles *Free Press*, was born at the Xanadu, which was, among other things, the home for disaffected journalists who worked at places like the Los Angeles *Times*. Muns had worked at community papers. The guy who actually started the *Free Press* rather than just talking about it was Art Kunkin, who had nothing to do with the rest of us. He had been the business manager of the *Militant*, the Trotskyite paper. He understood the difference between talking about publishing a newspaper and actually getting one out and in the readers' hands. Out of the *Free Press* came writers like Charles Bukowski. The Xanadu was also a popular venue for musicians like Sonny Terry, Brownie McGee, Hoyt Axton, Judy Collins, Pete Seeger and Cisco Houston and such counterculture heroes of the time such as LSD guru Owsley Stanley III. The Xanadu closed in 1963, partly because many of the Xanadu regulars went South to register voters during the civil rights battles of the time.

Muns was later a regular on Les Claypool Jr.'s popular radio show on KRHM-FM, a predecessor station of K-EARTH. Claypool's show introduced Phil Ochs and Bob Dylan to the Southland.

For many years Muns lived on the south slope of the Sierra and along the Northern California coast above San Francisco where he published poetry.

"Walden Muns was a first rate poet who took his gift lightly, as

*The beloved Girlie*

*Rosie and Greg Ahouse, son of John Ahouse, one of the two main editors on this book, were healthy, happy specimens in the last year of their lives. Now they are gone.*

*Nigey and Lionel in happier times*

*The author in 1997 at Skylight Books,*
*shortly after Nigey left him*

he did most things. He had a wild streak in the western spirit and was one of the great unacknowledged Beats of our times," said Bruce Cook, author of *The Beat Generation*, and former book editor of the Los Angeles *Daily News* and *USA Today*.

I miss Muns so. I miss Nigey and Girlie and Rosie.

No, 1997 was not a good year for the author personally. Yet he still remains convinced that the next milennium will somehow nourish the cause of progress, and not an unremitting under-the-volcano kind of plunge into another Dark Ages.

This book was set in 10 point Bodoni on 12 point leading and 3,000 copies were printed on acid-free 60 pound paper at McNaughton & Gunn, Inc. in Saline, Michigan.